ROSALIE BERTELL

WOMEN WHO ROCK series

ROSALIE BERTELL

Scientist, Eco-Feminist, Visionary

MARY-LOUISE ENGELS

Women's Press
Toronto

Rosalie Bertell: Scientist, Eco-Feminist, Visionary
by Mary-Louise Engels

First published in 2005 by
Women's Press, an imprint of Canadian Scholars' Press Inc.
180 Bloor Street West, Suite 801
Toronto, Ontario
M5S 2V6

www.womenspress.ca

Canadian Scholars' Press/Women's Press gratefully acknowledges financial support for our publishing activities from the Ontario Arts Council, the Canada Council for the Arts, the Government of Canada through the Book Publishing Industry Development Program (BPIDP), and the Government of Ontario through the Ontario Book Publishing Tax Credit Program.

Library and Archives Canada Cataloguing in Publication

Engels, Mary-Louise
Rosalie Bertell : scientist, eco-feminist, visionary / Mary-Louise Engels.

ISBN 0-88961-450-4

1. Bertell, Rosalie 1929– 2. Environmentalists—Canada—Biography. 3. Epidemiologists—Canada—Biography. 4. Radioactive pollution—Health aspects. I. Title.

HD9698.C22B47 2005   363.7'0092   C2004-906140-2

Cover design, text design and layout: Susan Thomas/DigitalZone
Cover photograph: Rosalie Bertell in 1980 (Rosalie Bertell's collection)

05 06 07 08 09   5 4 3 2 1

Printed and bound in Canada by AGMV Marquis Imprimeur Inc.

ONTARIO ARTS COUNCIL
CONSEIL DES ARTS DE L'ONTARIO

THE CANADA COUNCIL   LE CONSEIL DES ARTS
FOR THE ARTS   DU CANADA
SINCE 1957   DEPUIS 1957

Canadä

CONTENTS

Dr. Rosalie Bertell can identify the precise evening in 1973 when her life changed forever. At a village meeting near Buffalo, New York, she faced an expectant audience. The people of Lockwood had gathered to hear about a proposal to build a nuclear reactor nearby. Rosalie, an epidemiologist, biometrician, and nun, spoke to them calmly and convincingly about the hazards of low-level radiation. She described her research linking X-rays to the onset of leukemia, then turned to medical reports of cancer deaths and increasing numbers of low-birth-weight infants near a nuclear facility in Michigan. Her message was clear. Shortly afterward, the citizens of Lockwood voted down the reactor proposal. "So I started off with a victory," she recalls.

That day in Lockwood, Rosalie took the first major step toward her new role as anti-nuclear activist. The main elements of her future calling were all there: pointing out flaws in the narrative spun by an exceedingly well-financed nuclear indus-try determined to win public agreement for its continued expansion; warning about the health risks of a little-understood technology; joining with other citizens, particularly women, in a fight against powerful opponents; and advancing the claims of infants to safe and healthy surroundings.

Harnessing nuclear energy for war and peace was arguably the most momentous event of the twentieth century. Nuclear weapons changed the face of war and peace forever, ushering in an era in which all-out war became "impossible," while the costs of permanent preparations for war reached unprecedented heights.

Nuclear energy promised a means of spreading progress and prosperity worldwide, powered by electricity that was safe, clean, and cheap. The hazards associated with nuclear energy, however, were at first imperfectly understood and systematically concealed. During the second half of the 20th century, the terrifying prospect gradually emerged that this new technology, and the poisonous wastes it leaves behind, could destroy life on the planet.

For many years, the US government maintained tight control over the nuclear story. The US Army of Occupation in post-Hiroshima Japan controlled research on radiation effects and censored writing, photographs, and films about those affected by the first bombs, both living and dead. An entrenched policy of obscuring the truth about radiation effects was to leave many victims in its wake: uranium miners in Canada's north, workers in the nuclear weapons and nuclear power industries, and residents of communities adjoining those facilities. Soldiers exposed to radiation in Hiroshima and Nagasaki and to fallout from nuclear tests, indigenous peoples in the Pacific, Americans living downwind from Nevada test sites, and many others faced disease, disability, and death. So will their descendants, doubly jeopardized by genetic damage and by the continuing presence in the environment of long-lived radioactive contamination. As knowledge grew about radiation effects, safety hazards, and the insolubility of the nuclear waste problem, Canadian and American citizens began demanding greater accountability of governments and industry.

Rosalie was among the many scientists, scholars, and activists who struggled for decades to uncover and publicize the secrets of radioactivity. A citizen of the United States, Canada, and the world, she was determined to see beyond the official narratives about nuclear energy. The mission she set for herself was to bring to public attention the effects of radiation on past, present, and future generations—to "make the victims visible." In 2004, the viability of the powerful nuclear industry in the Western world seems uncertain. And Rosalie, at age 75, looks back at over 30 years spent as a redoubtable critic of the powerful nuclear industry, and consequently as the object of censorship, vilification, and threat.

This book tells her story.

CHAPTER I

A BECKONING WORLD

Only six days after her birth in 1929, Rosalie Bertell was stricken with pneumonia. Her parents, Paul and Helen, had lost their first child, a son, in infancy, and for a time they feared that their third of four children, Rosalie, might not survive either. With care and attention she did, but that dangerous early bout with pneumonia was only the first of many such episodes in a childhood and adulthood ravaged by illness. Fortunately, Rosalie had a strong and supportive family that handled her health problems with sensitivity while encouraging her strengths—and there were many.

Rosalie's father, Paul Bertell, was a fourth-generation American from New Jersey, of German, Austrian, and French ancestry. Her mother, Helen Twohey Bertell, a fourth-generation Irish Canadian from Port Colborne, Ontario, had moved to Buffalo when her father, a physician, became chief of staff at the Providence Retreat Hospital. Thus, from birth, Rosalie enjoyed dual American and Canadian citizenship. Helen and Paul met at the hospital when he visited his aunt Rosalie Wolfe, a Daughter of Charity and the hospital pharmacist. Both as a nun and as a health professional, Aunt Rosalie was an important role model for the child who was named after her.

The Buffalo in which Rosalie grew up was an important centre of shipping, industry, and manufacturing, and a city with close ties to the Ontario heartland, a short distance away.

The vibrant metropolis boasted four daily newspapers, five legitimate theatres, and a population exceeding one million. Located on the shores of Lake Erie, it was adorned by architectural gems and beautiful parks, a legacy of the Pan-American Exposition held there in 1901. Originally attracting settlers because of its rich farmland, Buffalo became an important transportation hub during the 19th century when it was chosen as the beginning of the Erie Canal.

The Bertells moved to Kenmore, north of Buffalo, when Rosalie was an infant, to Detroit when she was three, and back to Kenmore when she was six. The suburb of Kenmore had been established in the late 19th century as a community of upscale homes on tree-lined streets, a leafy retreat where residents could enjoy life free from the tumult of industrial Buffalo. The Bertells were a close-knit, pious family, and their lives centred on home, parish church, school, and work.

Perhaps they were drawn closer by Rosalie's uncertain health. "I missed one to two months of school every year until my last year in college," she recalls. "Usually it was pneumonia, scarlet fever, chicken pox, whooping cough, measles. I had my first pneumonia when I was six days old. The doctor told my mother to keep me home from school every once in a while just on general principle."

Rosalie's older sister, Mary Katherine, eventually became an art teacher. After her retirement, she helped Rosalie deal with her voluminous correspondence. Her brother, John Twohey Bertell, 17 months her junior, grew up to be a criminal lawyer and practised for many years in the Buffalo area. He was a sturdy source of support for Rosalie on the frequent occasions when she required legal or brotherly advice or reassurance.

The Legacy: Health, Activism, Enterprise

Rosalie was proud of a legacy of health professionals on both sides of the family. "My family has a history of involvement with the health professions, which dates back to my great-grandmother's origin in Baden, the centuries-old health spa in Austria," she recalls. "It includes generations of doctors, pharmacists, and nurses on both sides of my family." Her concern for the vulnerable and marginalized, along with her optimistic and practical spirit, she attributes to her parents' influence. Exploring the roots of her social activism, Rosalie often recounted how her mother noticed that Black women, after working all day in white homes, would stand for an hour or more waiting for a bus to take them home. If there were only Blacks at a corner, the buses did not stop. My mother went down every evening to stand with the Black women so that the buses would stop—until the drivers got the point."

Although the effects of the stock market crash in 1929 on the Bertell household were not dramatic, Rosalie says she feels, looking back, that her parents were apprehensive about the future. "I think they were frightened and very frugal. My father was never out of work. We never realized that my father was earning 'good money'! I thought we were poor. There was no big spending in our house when we were growing up." Her preference for a simple lifestyle and her ability to deal with periods of marginal income were established early.

She admired her father's ingenuity and his business acumen. "My father never finished high school, but taught himself very complicated math, physics, and optics," Rosalie recounts. "He became the president of a corporation, the Standard Mirror Company, where he invented the day–night automobile mirror. Later, he delighted in my success in math and everything I did." During her college vacations, Rosalie enjoyed working with her father, doing his 10-year financial projections, learning about the corporate business world, and absorbing something of his entrepreneurial drive.

School Days: Music, Mathematics, Religion

Rosalie has described herself as "constitutionally shy," but her illnesses, the resulting disruption in her school attendance, and her inability to participate fully in childhood games and activities must have contributed to this social reserve. Early shyness did not prevent her, however, from developing both a sense of humour and a personality that her many subsequent friends and admirers found warm and engaging. Nor did it inhibit her willingness—enraging to her future detractors—to express strong opinions in trenchant prose.

Early in her life, Rosalie discovered the pleasures of frequent solitude, independent learning, and compensatory achievement. Her ill health, and the sensitive manner in which her parents responded to it, shaped Rosalie's opportunities and personality from the outset. Her frail constitution meant that she was under no pressure to conform to the social values of her peers, and could concentrate instead on developing strengths of mind and spirit. At the same time, it is likely that her abiding concern for the vulnerable, and particularly for the imperiled health of women and children, was born during those early years of sickness, and as a child of parents who had already lost one infant. Yet she never worried about her own health as a child. "I just thought it was the way things were."

When confined to home during the early school years, "I learned to teach myself so that I did not fall behind the rest of the class." After a severe illness at the end of the eighth grade, she was ordered by the doctor to sit in the backyard every day but not run around with the other children. "They stayed and played with me for a while, but then lost interest. My father brought me a book about chess experts, and I sat in the backyard by the hour and figured out all of the winning moves. I became the champion chess player in the family and neighbourhood."

Rosalie was recognized from childhood as both a promising musician and the local mathematical prodigy. She began piano lessons in fourth grade, adding violin and organ in high school. She played in the school orchestra, sang in the church choir, and during long family drives, kept up her spirits by singing hymns and composing poetry. In eighth grade, she organized her first political protest on a musical theme, after the class music teacher was transferred. Rosalie organized all the students to boycott music lessons unless the school brought their teacher back. "Finally, the principal brought our former teacher back, to ask us to accept the new teacher. She told us she did not have her state requirements, and had to be a temporary teacher until she finished. We gave in." In high school, after being cautioned to avoid undue physical exertion, she was in demand as a pianist for dances.

Her first and enduring academic love, however, was mathematics, which she credits with helping her to think logically and abstractly. After beginning first grade at a crowded parochial school in Detroit, she learned so quickly that when she returned to Kenmore that year, she found she was ahead of the other children. When her new teacher announced that they were going to start learning the "ands, froms, times, and goes-intos," Rosalie inquired whether she meant addition, subtraction, multiplication, and division. During high school, she chose mathematics as her major academic subject, resolving to get 100 percent in all of the New York State Regents' Exams in Mathematics—and she succeeded.

Rosalie also gave early signs of a devout nature. In particular, she was attracted by religious music. "The day I first got permission to walk to seven a.m. mass, my mother told me to receive communion and come right home. I received communion and was kneeling in the front row with my head in my hands praying, when a wonderful thing happened! The organ played and a beautiful singing voice in Latin was heard. I thought I was in heaven and stayed there enthralled. I don't know how long it was, but suddenly my brother appeared in church and pulled me out of the pew. Mother had sent him after me."

Signs of her future religious vocation emerged in childhood. "I knew from the time I was very young that I would enter the convent. I don't know why I was so sure." Rosalie recalls that she played with her dolls with "great dedication," somehow knowing that when she was older she would not have her own children. "The dolls were on regular schedules, and well cared for. When I felt the play time was over, I called the St. Vincent de Paul people to come and take all of my dolls away—even the small knitted shawls and layettes which my grandmother had made for them. Everyone was surprised."

Rosalie appears to have bypassed the joys and woes of adolescent dating rituals. "I did struggle with my love for babies and my desire to have some. I would ask God to help me with this if He/She really wanted me in the convent. I prayed for a boyfriend who would not be romantically interested in me—and God sent a wonderful friend. We went to all of the parties together and had great fun. I never had any regrets." In later years, that high school companion became an English and Drama teacher, and a world traveller. They remain good friends, and he has never married either. "And I get the blame for that!" she admits.

What did darken her high school years, however, was the news of the Second World War. The deaths in combat of local servicemen reflected the toll of casualties across the nation, as kamikaze planes wreaked havoc on the American Pacific fleet. The very existence of a highly lethal war challenged her beliefs about the goodness of the universe and the sacredness of human life. The victory achieved through atomic fire in Japan raised questions that would preoccupy her throughout her life.

The Bomb

With a violent flash that ripped the sky apart and a thunderous sound that shook the earth to its foundation, Hiroshima was pounded to the ground. In an instant, the city was reduced to ash and rubble. A fireball of several

million degrees centigrade formed, and from the inciner-
ated buildings rose a huge cloud of dust and ashes, cast-
ing the city in darkness .... Then from where a city once
was, a huge column of fire bounded straight up toward
heaven. A dense cloud of smoke rose and spread out,
covering and darkening the whole sky .... Fires broke out
all over and soon merged into a huge conflagration .... Out
of the fierce whirlwind, half-naked and stark naked bodies
darkly soiled and covered with blood began moving.

—*The Legacy of Hiroshima: Its Past, Our Future*
Naomi Shohno

The Manhattan Project to produce the atomic bomb in the
Second World War was centred at Los Alamos, New Mexico.
Evolving in an atmosphere of concealment, centralization,
and control, it was fuelled by the knowledge that German
scientists also were working on such a bomb.

The Project was built on a stunning 1939 publication by
two German physicists. Their paper announced that nuclear
fission—the splitting of the atom—not only was theoretically
possible, but had already taken place in the laboratory. They
revealed how the nucleus of a uranium atom could be split
when bombarded by neutrons, releasing tremendous energy
and throwing off more neutrons. These extra neutrons could

then cause additional uranium atoms to split, releasing even more energy and more neutrons. Thus, one fission could start a "chain reaction." Their work touched off a flurry of fission experiments in laboratories around the world.

One of the most complex scientific undertakings in history, the Manhattan Project coordinated facilities located in nineteen states and two Canadian provinces. Although it drew on basic scientific discoveries by European and British scientists, the Project's planners and personnel were mostly American, with some participation by British and Canadian scientists. Under wartime conditions of top secrecy, only a few scientists and military planners at the highest levels were permitted to see the whole picture. The existence of the Project was concealed from the US Congress, and even from the vice-president. On July 16, 1945, the first atomic bomb, code-named Trinity, was exploded at the test site in Alamogordo, New Mexico. "The idea was to explode the damned thing .... We weren't terribly concerned with the radiation," the project's deputy medical officer, Hymer Friedell, was later quoted as saying.

The following month, two atomic bombs were dropped: on Hiroshima, August 6, and on Nagasaki, August 9. The Hiroshima bomb was made from uranium mined in Canada and the Congo. The Nagasaki bomb was made from pluto-nium, a previously unknown element almost non-existent in nature, formed from uranium in nuclear reactors.

When a nuclear bomb explodes, it turns into a ball of energy five times hotter than the centre of the sun. At the same instant, dozens of different radioactive fission products are released, including such unstable radioactive isotopes as strontium-90, cesium-137, and iodine-131. Such fission products were unprecedented: they had never occurred in human food, air, or water before the first atomic bomb explosions. Thus, in addition to causing heat and blast effects, the nuclear explosions transmuted the very fabric of matter, emitting silent, invisible radiations that persisted long after the blast and fire were over.

The jubilant reaction to the bomb announcement in Rosalie's hometown typified the response across the nation. "The streets erupted with joy. My brother and a friend ran to the church, where I was practising the organ, and rang the bell for two hours, until they couldn't ring any more. The war was over! But when I came home, my mother was strangely subdued as she prepared supper, stirring a pot on the stove and repeating quietly, 'They shouldn't have done it. They shouldn't have done it.' How did she know at that time? That remark continued to haunt me."

Officially, however, the bombs were hailed as a triumph of American technological prowess. President Truman's announcement of the first bomb drop contained no mention of casualties nor of the bomb's most distinctive new feature: radiation. The bomb, he declared, demonstrated the might of an energy "harnessing the basic power of the universe," which would "supplement the growing power of our armed forces," help to maintain world peace, and become a potentially revolutionary source of energy. Almost everyone thought that the bombs were just extra-powerful forms of ordinary bombs—"just another piece of artillery," as Truman said, and justified by the need to end the war.

The war, Rosalie came to believe, never really ended. Driven by perceived threat from the USSR and a determination to maintain military dominance, the American government's development of nuclear weaponry continued apace. In 1949, the USSR acquired the bomb—and the massive nuclear arms build-up of the Cold War began.

By then, American bomb testing in the Pacific was in full swing. The first of 66 Pacific bomb tests started in 1946 and continued until 1958. Also in 1946, the first of over 1,000 nuclear tests in the United States itself began, mostly at the Nevada test site. The amount of radioactive fallout dumped over North America remained a secret for almost 50 years. Only slowly, and in the teeth of official secrecy and misrepresentation, did scientists begin to realize the human costs of testing.

From College Studies to Missile-Making

On graduating from high school, Rosalie won two scholarships: a music scholarship to a college in Rochester, New York, and a general academic scholarship to Margaret D'Youville College in Buffalo. The latter institution was named after the only Canadian-born saint, founder of the Order of the Grey Nuns of the Sacred Heart, which Rosalie would later join. At this time, her grandmother, partially paralyzed and blind, lived with the family and required special care. Since her mother needed help and her sister had begun teaching in another city, Rosalie remained in Buffalo and entered D'Youville, deciding to specialize in mathematics.

While at college, she studied diligently, held many elected offices in campus associations, and received her BA *magna cum laude* in 1950. But happiness eluded her. She could find no answers to preoccupations about the shape of her own future—nor about the state of a world darkened by nuclear testing, the onset of the undeclared Korean war in 1950, and the emergence of an anti-communist crusade propelled by Senator Joseph McCarthy.

Impelled by a need to feel more in touch with "inward spaces," she decided to join the Carmelites, a contemplative religious order for women, in Vermont. "I had the feeling that I needed to pull away, that I was so engrossed in activity that I was not understanding what was going on. It seemed right that I enter a Carmelite monastery. They're one of the most withdrawn of Catholic religious communities. You go in and your whole life is encompassed within their walls. Usually people don't ever come out for the rest of their lives." She had reached a turning point: for the first time, she was preparing to take a major step in opposition to her parents' wishes.

There had been priests and nuns in the family tree, and her parents did not oppose her entering religious life, especially as a teacher. But they feared that the taxing physical regimen of a Carmelite nun's life would jeopardize their daughter's delicate health. Rosalie, however, remained firm. "I thought I could do anything." Even a premonitory incident, when she donned for the first time the heavy habit worn by the Carmelites, did not deter her. "I could not get my breath," she recalls. "They debated whether or not I was strong enough to wear it."

Before she could enter the monastery, however, she needed $2,000, "the dowry you are asked to bring in order to enter —a great deal of money to me at the time." The dowry was a kind of insurance policy, in case a Sister ever had to leave the convent and needed financial support while she adjusted once again to the outside world. Rosalie had been raised to value paying her own way, so the hunt for a high-paying job was on. After a brief search, she found one: doing basic research on guided missile systems in the engineering department of Bell Aircraft.

For the quiet and studious young nun-to-be, it was a strange and exhilarating new world. After each trial flight, she worked on data analysis. "I had FBI security clearance, working in an office where armed people walked up and down between the desks. If you left your place during the day, you had to lock your papers in the desk drawer. Our Thermos bottles were examined at night when we left work, to see if we were carrying any papers out."

Despite the cloak-and-dagger atmosphere, the job appealed to her idealism. Employees considered themselves pioneers who were producing the benign, surgically accurate weapons of the future. The missiles would revolutionize war by targeting military objectives only, never again hitting hospitals or schools. "You were made to feel that you were doing a fine thing for humanity by inventing these bombs," says Rosalie. "And I believed all that."

During her high school and college years, Rosalie had often felt constrained to downplay her mathematical prowess. At Bell Aircraft, by contrast, she received plaudits for her mathematical skills and ingenuity. "I remember being very excited one time when a missile was shot off and they couldn't tell whether or not it had turned upside down during the test. If it had turned upside down, all the instruments were recording opposite to the usual orientation. I took that problem on as a special project and was able to save their doing one missile shot over again."

In later years, Rosalie often condemned the way in which so many gifted young people were co-opted into scientific careers funded by the military. Her experience of working on secret high-tech projects at Bell gave her lasting insight into how easy it was to be seduced: by the intellectual challenge, by applause for superior abilities, by misleading accounts of what was being done—and why. Years later in 1995, at an international women's conference in Beijing, she drew attention to the nuclear "brain drain," describing how young, intelligent students are

> captured for the secret military projects into which money and resources are poured. The nations undertaking such practices want to "harness technology" in the cause of world domination This brain drain has the effect of harming all civilian enterprises, including medical and educational services. It is difficult to obtain funding unless projects are related to some area in which there is military interest. It biases the economic and the intellectual efforts of society toward military priorities.

Joining the Carmelites

In September 1951, having accumulated her dowry, Rosalie took up her religious vocation. She was 22 years old. The Carmelite monastery was an imposing old house high on a grassy hill overlooking the town of Barre, Vermont. There, she sought a quiet life withdrawn from worldly strivings. The monastic life appealed to her as a way of changing the world by choosing a contemplative lifestyle in harmony with nature. She credits the experience as providing her with an enduring sense of the strengths developed through solitude and silent listening.

In contrast to what she'd experienced in her previous years of academic striving and competition, Rosalie found a haven in Carmel where only the present counted. "One is not trying to become accredited or pass tests or prepare for the future," she explained. "Today is richly present and precious. The work is co-operative, not competitive, and interpersonal problems are resolved, not ignored." Since the life at Carmel involved being with a small group of people, on one acre of land, for the rest of one's life, friendship with others was essential. "Many of the skills I now need to live peacefully in a global village were first developed in that microcosm of human problems." At first, the change seemed to benefit the self-described "overachiever." Her pulse rate slowed and her blood pressure went down.

The monastery was run by and for women, subsisting through the hands-on labour of its members. For Rosalie, it was a dramatic change in lifestyle. "We used to dig four-foot ditches and lay pipes to run our own irrigation system. I learned how to thread pipes and put them together and lay cement walks. I learned plumbing and basic electricity. I found out that women could be pretty self-sufficient." Her respect for feminine practical and managerial skills grew, along with her self-confidence. While she painted doors and fashioned hemp sandals, she had time to contemplate—to think about using mathematics to make missiles, about bombs exploding in the Pacific, about the apparent human predilection for destructiveness.

Life among the Carmelites was demanding, and not only because of the hard physical labour that was part of the day's routine. The regimen also included frequent fasting and lengthy periods of obligatory prayer. The day began at 5 a.m. in the winter and 4 a.m. (with a one-hour midday siesta) in the summer. In all, the nuns spent about eight hours a day in formal prayer, retiring at 11 p.m. After five years, Rosalie suffered an episode of congestive heart failure and had to leave the monastery on July 15, 1956. Certainly there was a heavy genetic loading of cardiac illness in her family: her mother, father, brother, and both grandmothers all had heart disease. But no one doubted that the monastic rigours had impaired Rosalie's health.

Nevertheless, the disciplined routine of the monastery left a lasting impression. "I learned in Carmel to keep a rhythm to the day. Some people think I work all the time, but they don't watch me. At Carmel, they pace themselves .... That's why I keep the evening quiet for music and reading and prayer."

She returned home for the rest of the summer, and in September began to instruct in Latin and business math at a local Catholic high school. "I wanted to try teaching to see if entering a teaching [religious] community would be a viable option." In the summer of the following year, 1957, she began a master's program at The Catholic University of America, in Washington, D.C., rooming with other grad students near the university. Once again, she embraced her financial independence. While her father paid for phone calls to family and flights home for the holidays, she says, "We made some money by selling supper to students who just had rooms or didn't like to cook." She finished her studies for the MA in the summer of 1958, and her actual graduation ceremonies followed in June 1959.

Becoming a Grey Nun

In September 1958, her health much improved, she entered another religious order, the Grey Nuns of the Sacred Heart, a community offering a routine that was less physically demanding than that at Carmel. The Grey Nuns' tradition of social work and teaching was one that Rosalie treasured. She took pride in their sturdy female independence, their global reach, their legacy of service to the sick, the poor, and the marginalized. The Grey Nuns, she says, "has a strong history

of health care and social work both in North America, origi-
nating in the General Hospital of Montreal about 1736, and
then globally. This history has obviously influenced my
concern for health."

The order was founded by a widowed mother of 29 with
two children. Marguerite D'Youville, for whom Rosalie's
alma mater in Buffalo had been named, ran a brewery to
finance a hospital, where she took care of Native peoples, as
well as French and British soldiers. With three other Sisters,
Marguerite also opened the first foundling home in North
America, where they cared for prostitutes, the elderly, and
others needing help. Unlike many other female religious
orders, the Grey Nuns never permitted male leadership. They
originally travelled to the West in covered wagons with the
settlers, and today serve in such areas as northern Canada,
South America, Asia, and Africa.

Rosalie remained a member of the Grey Nuns, and her
religious beliefs and commitments formed the bedrock
emotional and spiritual support for her daily life. Moreover,
developments within Catholicism strengthened her growing
passion for finding ways to right social wrongs. She often
referred to the inspiration she received from the early delib-
erations of the Second Vatican Council in 1962. At that time,
John Paul II and hundreds of bishops gathered in Rome to
redirect the course of the Catholic Church, emphasizing
involvement with the world.

She continued to live a cloistered life, residing with other nuns, but the Grey Nuns' rules were less stringent than those of the Carmelites. "Around 1968, we began to wear more appropriate clothes. Also the daily schedule was shortened, with many obligatory prayers in private, according to your best time for them. After Vatican II, active religious were to place top priority on ministry"—that is, the duty of service to others. Rosalie believes that most women religious welcomed the changes as allowing for more flexibility and a prayer life that is deeper because it is less regimented.

With the encouragement of her new order, Rosalie taught mathematics full time for four years at Sacred Heart Junior College in Pennsylvania. A new door opened in 1963, when the National Institute of Health offered her a grant to earn

her PhD in mathematics. At that time, there was a national program to shift mathematicians out of physics and chemistry and into biological applications. "I became interested in taking what I already knew," she explains, "and moving it into understanding living systems."

By examining processes such as homoeostasis—how the body maintains a stable temperature and a constant level of blood sugar——she learned to quantify complicated biological processes. One project, devising a kidney filter for screening out extraneous materials, gave her a sense of how the organism is perturbed by the introduction of something foreign. These kinds of learning were an important part of the scientific background she later brought to bear on the question of how radiation affects human organs and tissues. When she received her PhD in 1966, she won the award for outstanding graduate student in mathematics for the Washington, D.C. area. During her student years she was also awarded membership in the Kappa Gamma Pi Academic Honour Society, and the Sigma Xi Scientific Research Honour Society.

Throughout her graduate studies and afterwards, she taught in Philadelphia, Atlanta, and at D'Youville College in Buffalo. Rosalie loved students and the art of teaching. In particular, she delighted in devising innovative teaching materials to awaken students' confidence in their abilities to learn and enjoy mathematics, physics, chemistry, and biology. In 1973, she received an Outstanding Educator of America award.

As time passed, however, she could not shake feelings of frustration that she was not making use of her advanced research training in biometry. Moreover, the tensions of very large classes and disagreements over academic protocols touched off more episodes of illness. Never precisely diagnosed, her symptoms involved extremely low blood pressure and intense fatigue. She began shifting toward research, and left D'Youville College in 1973.

After leaving teaching, she began full-time work as a biometric researcher at an institute where she had worked part time since 1970: Roswell Memorial Institute in Buffalo, one of the world's top cancer research institutes. There she anticipated uninterrupted academic focus. Yet quiet seclusion, whether in laboratory or monastery, never quite worked out for Rosalie as a lifestyle. The claims of the outside world always beckoned her in new and unanticipated directions.

CHAPTER 2

THE REALM OF RADIATION

With a post-doctoral grant in hand, Rosalie was now a senior cancer research scientist at Roswell Memorial Park Institute. She joined a prestigious research project on leukemia, a cancer of the bone marrow that results in the uncontrolled overproduction of white blood cells. The study began in the early 1960s when a puzzling rise in the rate of leukemia had been observed in the northeastern United States. For several years, Rosalie and a multidisciplinary team of investigators examined the question: why is the leukemia rate increasing?

The Tri-State Leukemia Survey

The Tri-State Leukemia Survey, the largest of its kind ever undertaken to that date, examined the incidence of leukemia in Maryland, New York, and Minnesota. Involving a population of six million, the survey had gathered many kinds of information about its subjects—on socioeconomic class, health history, race, occupation, medical history, and more—and then waited to see what happened with respect to leukemia.

"When I was hired, the data had been collected and computerized but evaluation was just beginning," Rosalie recalls. "After examining many variables, it became obvious to me and everyone else on the team that the really strong effect, the leukemia effect, was coming from diagnostic medical X-rays." These X-rays emitted the very low levels of ionizing radiation that for years had been dismissed as harmless. Rosalie analyzed the data on adult subjects. Her major conclusion was that "by using X-rays, we were increasing leukemia by accelerating body breakdown, aging. The person could no longer fight it off. The leukemia rate is high at both ends of the age scale. Very young children, whose immune system is not yet operating fully, are vulnerable to it, as are the elderly. The leukemia rate reaches a low point at age 15 and then it gradually goes up for the rest of life." What X-ray exposures did, in her view, was to hasten the process of biological entropy.

The idea that radiation contributes to aging was not new. Indeed, biologists had long believed that the natural radiation with which we are all surrounded from birth onwards is one of the major causes of human aging. Rosalie concluded that her research had demonstrated this relationship mathematically and established a link with X-ray use. "I found that the rate of leukemia went up like compound interest about 5.3 percent per year, just by living. It also went up at a rate of about 4 to 5 percent for trunk X-rays. You could see the leukemia rate go up with each chest or spinal X-ray."

Her colleagues on the Tri-State Survey also found strong X-ray radiation effects when they analyzed the data on children. Dr. Irwin Bross and Dr. Nachimuthu Natarajan found that children of mothers X-rayed during pregnancy suffered 1.5 times the leukemia rate of children of mothers not X-rayed. In certain subcategories, exposed groups were 5 to 25 times more likely to develop leukemia than the general population.

Pioneering Studies of X-rays and Cancer

The Tri-State Survey was not the first to report findings that questioned the safety of low-dose ionizing radiation emanating from X-rays. In 1958, Dr. Alice Stewart published in the *British Medical Journal* her path-breaking study of childhood cancer. Based on extensive interviews with mothers throughout England about their experiences during pregnancy, Dr. Stewart, a British physician and epidemiologist, found that fetal X-rays doubled a child's risk of developing cancer. Her work was for years derided, attacked, or ignored by the medical and scientific establishment. Critics argued in particular that her study was flawed by its reliance on mothers' memories about their medical histories. "In spite of attempts to cut her research funds and weary her spirit," Rosalie commented, "Alice

Stewart continued methodically to prove her points about the seriousness of human exposure to radiation."

Intrigued by Stewart's findings, Dr. Brian MacMahon, an epidemiologist at Harvard's School of Public Health, carried out a study of 37 maternity hospitals in New England, using hospital X-ray records instead of mothers' accounts. He confirmed Stewart's results, eventually finding that cancer mortality was 40 percent higher among children whose mothers had been X-rayed. A significant feature of this research was the lapse of time between exposure to X-rays and the onset of cancer. In fact, having observed no cancer among the children after eight years of investigation, MacMahon initially wrote up these negative findings for publication. But in the last year of the study, the leukemia cases began appearing and he had to rewrite his paper, highlighting the long time lag between exposure to radiation and the appearance of illness.

As a study of a very large and diverse population, the Tri-state Survey was important in confirming previous findings by Dr. Stewart and Dr. MacMahon of a relationship between X-ray exposure and cancer. Such results, raising serious issues about permissible levels of radiation from medical X-rays, endeared Bertell and her colleagues neither to the medical profession, nor to the regulatory bodies that established "safe" levels of exposure to radiation.

The Tri-State research introduced Rosalie to the world of

radiation and its effects on human life. Her previous studies in physics, chemistry, and biology had touched on the subject of radiation, the propagation of energy through space or tissue in the form of waves or particles. Having specialized in mathematics, however, she had much to discover about ionizing radiations, which can disrupt the atoms and molecules within the body.

Ionizing radiation refers to radiation at the high-energy end of the electromagnetic radiation spectrum. It encompasses not only X-rays, but also the forms of radiation associated with nuclear energy: alpha and beta particles, gamma rays, and neutrons. Rosalie set out to absorb what was known. Eventually she wrote a major work on the topic, *No Immediate Danger: Prognosis for a Radioactive Earth* (Women's Press, 1986), which publicized the dangers of radiation to the world.

Radiation Physics: The Basics

Atoms, the basic building blocks of matter, consist of comparatively large particles (protons and neutrons) clustered in a central nucleus, orbited by smaller particles (electrons): a miniature "solar system." Normally, atoms are electrically stable: the number of positively charged protons in the centre equals the number of negatively charged electrons in orbit. The number of neutrons may vary.

An ion is any atom or molecule that does not have the normal number of electrons. Losing one or more electrons gives an atom an electrical charge, a process called ionization. Two electrically charged particles, or ions, are created by this process: the negatively charged electron and the rest of the atom that now has a positive electrical charge. Ionizing radiation, therefore, is any form of radiation that has enough energy to knock electrons out of atoms or molecules, creating ions. Ionized atoms are very unstable and prone to form new combinations with other atoms and molecules.

The number of protons in an atom determines what element it is. When atoms have the same number of protons, but different numbers of neutrons, they are different "isotopes," or "nuclides," of the same element. Isotopes, then, are variant forms of an element, distinguished by their differing numbers of neutrons. Thus, uranium-234 (U-234), uranium-235 (U-235), and uranium-238 (U-238) are different isotopes of uranium.

Some heavy atoms, such as uranium, are naturally unstable and constantly disintegrating. Such atoms are radioactive; that is, they emit radiation spontaneously. As they disintegrate, they give off radiation in the form of alpha and beta particles, and gamma waves. These radiations travel with such energy that they can knock electrons out of any atom with which they collide. The biological damage they cause results from their ability to ionize atoms, disrupting the body's molecular structure. The effect of ionizing radiation on the living cell is like that of "a madman loose in a library," in the words of US health physics pioneer Dr. Karl Z. Morgan.

Alpha particles lose their energy quickly and do not penetrate the surface of the skin when exposed externally. However, they can enter the body through a cut in the skin, by ingestion, or by inhalation, and are extremely harmful once inside, ionizing atoms and disrupting living cells. Uranium, plutonium, and radium are all alpha emitters (sources of alpha radiation). Plutonium, as Rosalie repeatedly warned, is a particularly potent alpha emitter. "No quantity inhaled has been found to be too small to induce lung cancer in animals."

Beta particles can penetrate a metre or so of air and the first layers of skin in human beings. Iodine-131 and strontium-90, for example, are beta emitters. Iodine-131, a radioactive by-product of fission created during nuclear explosions and in nuclear reactors, can be inhaled and ingested. Iodine-131 may damage or destroy thyroid cells, and increase the risk of thyroid cancer. Strontium-90, an isotope chemically similar to calcium, collects in the bones and irradiates the bone marrow where white blood cells are formed.

Gamma rays and X-rays, with no electrical charge and no mass, do not interact with matter unless they actually collide directly with an atom and ionize it. Theoretically, a single "hit" of radiation to an atom can destroy the cell of which that the atom is a part, but a cell's chances of being destroyed increase as more of its atoms are ionized.

The biological effect of radiation may be to kill the cell outright, or to alter its DNA code in a way that leaves the cell alive but with an error in its DNA blueprint—a mutation. Cancers may result from mutations in somatic cells (non-germ cells), and heritable (genetic) changes may result from mutations in germ cells (eggs and sperm). Human cells are equipped with DNA repair mechanisms that are able to detect and correct problems, but those mechanisms can be overwhelmed. Rosalie sums up these biological effects succinctly. "The gradual breakdown of human bio-regulatory integrity through ionizing and breakage of the DNA molecules," she writes, "gradually makes a person less able to tolerate environmental changes, and less able to recover from diseases or illness."

Researchers still do not fully understand the cellular changes caused by ionization. It should be remembered that the structure of DNA itself was not elucidated until 1953, long after the onset of studies into the effects of radiation on human beings. There is agreement, however, that cells are most sensitive to damage when they are dividing. Fetuses and growing children, therefore, are especially vulnerable.

The isotopes (or nuclides) of uranium, plutonium, iodine, and strontium mentioned above, along with many others, are naturally unstable or radioactive. Hence, they are called radionuclides. Their nuclei are constantly degenerating— giving off alpha, beta, or gamma radiation until they have achieved a stable state. As they emit radiation, they change, or decay, into different isotopes. The more unstable an isotope, the faster it decays.

Every radioactive isotope has its own "physical half-life," which is the time required for half of the atoms of the isotope to decay to a different form. The breakdown of uranium-238, for example, produces a small amount of alpha radiation and a large amount of decay product. It takes about 4.5 billion years for one-half of the uranium-238 to break down. During the decay process, the parent uranium-238, its decay products, and their subsequent decay products release a series of new elements and radiation. In human terms, the half-life of uranium is forever. By contrast, the half-life of strontium-90 is 28 years, while that of iodine-131 is eight days.

The body also eliminates radioactive chemicals at different rates. The "biological half-life" refers to the time required for the body to eliminate one-half of the quantity of a radioactive chemical. Thus, the severity of health effects depends in part on how long the radioactive chemical remains in the body. "Radioactive cesium," Rosalie explains, "lodges in the muscles and is probably completely eliminated from the body in two years. Radioactive strontium lodges in bone and remains there for a lifetime, constantly irradiating the surrounding cells."

Radiation Technology:
X-rays, Bombs, Nuclear Power Plants

At the turn of the 20th century, three scientific breakthroughs heralded the onset of the radiation age. With the discovery of X-rays in 1895 by William Roentgen, the first modern application of ionizing radiation was born. The ability to see inside the human body for the first time seemed a medical miracle, and within a year, physicians were using X-rays for diagnosis and treatment. This initial marvel was quickly followed by Henri Becquerel's discovery of the radioactivity of uranium in 1896 and by Marie Curie's discovery of radium in 1898. Inexperienced practitioners and a hopeful public were quick to embrace X-rays and other radioactive emanations as wonder-working techniques and remedies.

During that century, X-rays were used to treat over 100 ailments, and radioactive radium treatments were prescribed or marketed as well, in radioactive skin cream, tooth paste, and bottled water. X-ray machines were installed in shoe stores to check shoe fit, and in beauty parlours to remove unwanted facial hair. Factory girls painted luminous dials on watches with radium, sucking their brushes to a fine point as they did so, and travellers in search of wonder cures inhaled radioactive radon gas in deep mines. The history of X-rays and of nuclear energy alike expose an eagerness to rush forward and use new technologies with little understanding of possible effects.

For over 100 years now, however, knowledge has accumulated about the negative effects of radiation exposure on human biology. German and Czech miners in the 19th century were known to suffer what was called "mountain sickness." By 1897, it had been demonstrated clinically that over half of the German miners working in the uranium-rich ores of the Erz mountains were dying of lung cancer, a disease almost unknown among the surrounding population. Many early physicians who used radiation received burns that would not heal, requiring amputation of their fingers and arms. Others developed fatal cancers, which continue to be an occupational hazard to radiologists today. Clients who tried out radium-based treatments and nostrums, especially in large doses, suffered appalling burns, painful ulcerations, and cancer. William Roentgen died from bone cancer and Madame Curie of leukemia. The harrowing illnesses and early deaths of many young dial painters taught the grim lesson that ionizing radiations do not pass straight through the body when eaten or inhaled, as had been previously believed. Instead, they accumulate in various organs, continually irradiating and damaging the surrounding cells.

This substantial body of anecdotal lore about the destructive effects of radiation was bolstered by experimental evidence in 1926. In that year, Hermann Muller demonstrated through animal experiments that radiation produced genetic mutations, research for which he eventually received the Nobel Prize. In 1928, the International Congress of Radiology began to issue internationally agreed-upon safety guidelines. These were remarkably precise and authoritative, given that knowledge about the hazards of radiation and how best to protect against it was still in its infancy.

The topic began to receive more scrutiny with the onset of the Manhattan Project, although findings about radiation effects, initially wartime secrets, were closely guarded. As a new era opened in the radiation story, US authorities consistently concealed, minimized, or lied about radiation effects from atomic blasts, weapons production, bomb testing, and nuclear power plants. The nuclear elite in government, industry, and regulatory bodies did not dispute the dangers of high-dose radiation, the kind that literally evaporated all life in its path. However, they continued to maintain that low-dose radiation posed no significant risk to human health, whether it emanated from bomb testing, reactors, or X-rays.

This was the contention that Rosalie Bertell spent the most productive part of her career in combatting.

Opposing the Nuclear Narrative

Rosalie's warnings about the health hazards of nuclear and X-ray technology built on the dissent of scientific critics who began raising radiation safety concerns shortly after the end of the Second World War. At that time, atomic bomb testing, first in the Pacific and later in Nevada, prompted the first strong opposition to the official story about radioactive emissions. Physicians and other scientists were prominent in this movement, since contesting the authorized line required a certain level of technical expertise. In the 1950s, several eminent scientists challenged the contention of the Atomic Energy Commission (AEC) that hazards from radioactive fallout were insignificant. Among these early dissidents were Hermann Muller, the Nobel Prize–winning radiation scientist, and the geneticist Edward B. Lewis, who was the first to suggest that iodine-131 was a hazard to the thyroid glands of children.

Linus Pauling, winner of the 1954 Nobel Prize in chemistry, warned that weapons testing would produce millions of birth defects, embryonic and neonatal deaths, and cancers. "Each nuclear test spreads the added burden of radioactive elements over every part of the world. Each added amount of radiation causes damage to the health of human beings all over the world and causes damage to the pool of human germ plasm such as to lead to an increase in the number of seriously defective children that will be born in future generations." He sent letters to scientists around the world, asking them to join him in an appeal, and got signatures from over 11,000 scientists demanding an end to testing, which he presented to the UN. His petition was a major influence in persuading the United States and USSR to agree to the 1963 moratorium on above-ground nuclear testing. Grilled before the House Un-American Activities Committee, he became an outcast at the California Institute of Technology, and eventually resigned from his university. He was one of the first scientists to lose his academic mooring after opposing the official "line." In the late 1970s, Rosalie Bertell would become another.

However, as Rosalie reflected on her findings in 1974, she anticipated only that they might arouse opposition from the medical profession, who would dispute her conclusion that X-ray exposure was hazardous to health. What she could not foresee was that the study would put her on a collision course with the nuclear power lobby.

Nuclear power development was an outgrowth of the push to produce the nuclear bomb. After the war, the United States and Canada were left with extensive research and production facilities and highly trained personnel. The reactors that transformed uranium into plutonium for bombs produced tremendous heat. Why not adapt them to boil water to turn turbines to generate electricity? "It's a hell of a way to boil water," remarked author Karl Grossman, "but it did keep the machinery running." To many, the idea also seemed like a redemptive opportunity to put the secrets of the atom to constructive use.

Using nuclear fission to produce electricity was one of the more sober ideas afloat in the current of hopeful predictions about a golden Atomic Age. Seers and scientists in the US foresaw individual atomic power plants for the home, atomic trains speeding through vacuum tubes at 10,000 miles per hour, atomic bombs melting the polar ice caps to produce a warmer climate, and atomic "artificial suns" to end bad weather forever. In 1952, President Dwight Eisenhower announced his Atoms for Peace policy, designed to demonstrate that nuclear fission and radiation were not heralds of illness and death but powerful helpers. This program aimed to present the friendly face of nuclear fission, and to argue that nuclear power reactors should be developed with tax dollars to generate clean, safe, cheap electricity—at home and abroad.

With massive financial support from the taxpayer, the nuclear power industry in the United States developed rapidly. At the apex of the nuclear hierarchy was the powerful Atomic Energy Commission (AEC). Established both to promote nuclear development and to regulate it, the AEC was in a conspicuous conflict of interest from the start, manifested by its consistent neglect of regulation in favour of aggressive nuclear development. By the 1960s, a seemingly viable industry was in place, and by 1974, when Rosalie joined the fray, the industry was burgeoning.

That year, President Nixon outlined a plan to build 1,000 reactors by the year 2000, and in one location after another, the industry followed a carefully crafted growth strategy. New sites for reactors were typically chosen in rural areas and small towns near large cities, since easy access to a significant market made economic sense. But, despite ritualistic claims that significant radiation hazards from plant effluents and major reactor accidents could not happen, there was no wish to test these assumptions in a populous metropolitan centre, nor to face the level of intellectual scrutiny that might arise from a sophisticated urban populace. Rather, the industry, bolstered by high-powered public relations initiatives, was successful in quietly persuading small communities to enjoy improved tax bases and local employment opportunities, while building the electricity resources of the future. Typically, industry representatives would present the advantages of nuclear power—safe, clean, cheap—to a local audience, respond to questions, and await the grant of a licence.

Confrontation and Fallout

This peaceful process of expansion was shattered in Niagara County, New York, in 1974. A citizens' group telephoned Roswell Institute, asking if someone was available to talk about the health effects of low-level radiation at a public meeting near Buffalo regarding a proposed nuclear power plant. No news of this proposal had appeared in the Buffalo newspapers. Rosalie, unaware that this meeting was to be a pivotal point in her career, agreed to go.

The forum had been organized by the New York State Electric & Gas Company. On the appointed evening, more than 200 citizens, along with county legislators, packed the meeting room at the local community college in Lockport. "When we went in the back door of the auditorium," Rosalie recounts, "we were handed a piece of paper containing questions the legislators had asked. It seems the utility company had had the questions for two weeks."

They were then given programs listing the names and expertise, followed by a blank space marked "Citizens' Energy Committee." "That was the four of us. Our names were not listed, and none of our credentials were given." Next, Rosalie says, she discovered that there were only enough chairs on the stage for the men from the utility company. The committee was asked to sit in the audience.

Five spokesmen for the electric utility delivered polished presentations, enhanced with "high-powered movies of nice, clean-looking nuclear power plants, with everything done by remote control." Rosalie noted particularly that the speakers dismissed radiation effects from reactor emissions as trivial, "no more serious than a few X-rays." The men's speeches, replete with technical jargon, were greeted by the audience with silence.

When Rosalie was called as the first speaker for the citizens' group, she strode to the stage and requested that the men give up their seats to the group. Then, observing for the first time that all members of the citizens' group were women, she remarked: "It's too bad that we have split this way on the issue. Maybe it is concern for life." She got a standing ovation from the audience, which was on her side from that moment.

At that point of her career, she claimed no special expertise on nuclear reactors. What she did have to impart, however, was what she had learned about low-level radiation effects from the study of X-rays and leukemia. How could the nuclear advocates be so certain that releasing radioactivity from reactor operations would carry no health risks? On that issue, she shared what she had learned from Dr. Gerald Drake, an internist who worked near the Big Rock Nuclear Plant, close to a resort and farming area near Charlevoix, Michigan. Dr. Drake had become concerned about changes he was observing in local public health indicators. Comparing local county records with those for the whole state, he had found statistically significant increases in the number of cancer deaths and low birth weights in Charlevoix.

"What really tipped the balance on the issue," she reported later, "was that next to this [proposed] power plant was the Cornucopia Farms where they grow Gerber's baby food." Shortly afterwards, the Niagara County legislature voted a moratorium against nuclear power, one of the first in the United States to do so. The moratorium prevented the construction of the nuclear plant. According to Rosalie, the possible threat that such a facility might have posed to the safety of food grown for babies was the critical factor in the citizens' vote.

The reactions to her speech surprised her. The telephone

began ringing with messages of congratulations and requests for speeches and public appearances. The negative fallout, however, was disconcerting. An attack letter headlined "Roswell Disavows Scientist" appeared almost immediately in the Lockport newspaper. A letter of retraction followed, after her department chairman, Dr. Irwin Bross, wrote to the newspaper in her defence.

More troubling were the criticism and censorship she began to experience at the Institute. When she mentioned that she had been invited to speak on a local television talk show, the hospital directors called her in to explain the Institute's policy about speaking on TV. Accompanied by Dr. Bross, whom she had asked to attend as a witness, Rosalie faced an hour of grilling. "They were really uptight, especially the assistant direc-tor, who spoke about how terrible it was to cause trouble in the local community and speak in the name of the hospital. When he finished, I asked him if he was trying to tell me that when I do research at public expense, and then go to a public meet-ing, I shouldn't tell the public what I've found out. This ques-tion so frustrated him that he walked out of the room and slammed the door." This episode highlighted what many of Rosalie's future critics would learn. Despite a quiet and unas-suming manner, she was an intrepid opponent, skilled at enlisting support, resourceful in verbal exchange.

The encounter with the nuclear power industry, and the overreaction to her own remarks made her uneasy. The feeling that "they were working too hard to keep me quiet" prompted her to find out as much as she could about the question that now preoccupied her. Who decides "permissible" dose levels of radiation?

Setting the Limits: "This time, folks, we've got it right!"

Rosalie began to study the history of federal regulations. She looked at where the utility companies were getting the information they were giving people on radiation questions, and found that most of it was coming from the American military experience at Hiroshima and Nagasaki. "In 1945, shortly after the bomb was dropped," says Rosalie, "the Americans set up the Atomic Bomb Casualty Commission (ABCC) in both cities and the government has kept total control of the information on radiation effects ever since. The data base is not released to the scientific community."

In launching her investigation into where the nuclear power officials were getting their information on radiation standards, Rosalie began pursuing the most sensitive and hotly debated issue about nuclear technology. What amounts of radiation are safe? The fact that this debate evolved in an atmosphere of secrecy and misinformation hobbled scientific understanding and public awareness for decades. It remains unresolved today.

Concealment, initially justified by the demands of war, was later maintained by concerns that radiation poisoning of Japanese citizens might be judged inhumane, like poison gas, or that victims might at some future date demand compensation. There were other reasons to minimize radiation effects. In the same years that the Hiroshima data were being interpreted, the Atomic Energy Commission in the United States was promoting the development of nuclear energy and defending bomb testing. There was no wish to fan public controversy about radiation hazards. From the start, the radiation debate was politicized.

The Atomic Bomb Casualty Commission (ABCC), later renamed the Radiation Effects Research Foundation (RERF), was established in 1947. Actual studies of the Japanese population did not begin until 1950, when many early deaths and miscarriages from radiation effects had already occurred. The scientists involved in this commission were primarily physicists, health physicists, and radiobiologists. Epidemiologists, who study patterns of illness in human populations, were not included, and there have been few biologists, geneticists, oncologists, pediatricians, or specialists in occupational health. Bountifully funded, the data gatherers produced many volumes of official reports. However, unlike scientific reports open for all scientists to scrutinize, these documents were reserved for a small number of approved scientists and regulators.

At the apex of the international regulatory system that

evolved is the International Commission on Radiation Protection (ICRP), which bases its standards on the RERF studies of the Japanese survivor population. A forerunner of the present organization, as previously noted, was formed in the late 1920s. After the war, the ICRP was transformed by an infusion of physicists who had worked on the Manhattan Project. It became the international arbiter on radiation safety standards, issuing recommendations that are not binding, but are, for the most part, followed by other national and international regulatory bodies.

Using the atomic bomb data as a base, the ICRP proceeded on the assumption, increasingly contested, that if you control the dose of radiation and spread it over time, risk becomes negligible. By 1976, its members acknowledged that all exposure carried some degree of risk. They argued, however, that "acceptable" or "permissible" levels of risk, balanced by the benefits of nuclear technology, could be arrived at. The lay public has found it difficult to grasp that "permissible" does not mean "safe." Rosalie became prominent among those who argued that determining the acceptability of such risk–benefit ratios was a social or political choice, not a scientific one, and that those who assumed the risks should have a voice in making that judgment: no radiation without representation.

Throughout its post-war history, ICRP members have been predominantly associated with the military and with medical radiological societies, all of which had vested interests in promoting the use of radiation and downplaying its risks. Rosalie, who became one of the commission's most vocal critics, later described it as "a self-perpetuating committee right out of the military .... It is, in every sense of the term, a closed club and not a body of independent scientific experts." Dr. Karl Morgan, himself a founding member of the ICRP, agrees that there has been a systemic bias in favour of special interest groups, thus making conflict of interest an unavoidable aspect of the standard-setting process. "I'm not sure it's an organization I would trust with my life," he stated.

Radiation Measurements

Radiological measurements are of three main kinds. There is measurement of radioactivity; measurement of exposure, that is, the amount of radiation received by a person; and measurement of the biological effects of radiation.

Curie (Ci): A measure of radioactivity. One curie undergoes 37 billion atomic disintegrations per second. This is the amount of radioactivity present in one gram of radium-226. Replaced by the Becquerel (Bq), representing 1 atomic disintegration per second.

Rad: A measurement of the amount of radiation received by a person. Rad stands for Radiation Absorbed Dose. Replaced by the Gray (Gy) (1 gray = 100 rad).

> Rem: A measurement of the biological effect of radiation. This unit takes into account that different forms of ionizing radiation have different biological impacts. A given amount of alpha radiation, for example, is approximately 10 times more biologically effective than the same amount of gamma radiation. Thus, one rad of alpha radiation translates into 10 rems, whereas one rad of gamma radiation equals only one rem. Replaced by the Sievert (Sv) ($1\,Sv = 100$ rem).

The measurement of radiation is complex, and the new measurement system, commemorating eminent figures in the history of radiation science, is not yet universally employed. These changes in terminology, and the fact that both sets of terms continue to be used, contribute to the difficulty that the average citizen experiences in attempting to understand the debate on "safe" doses of radiation. Another factor contributing to lay bewilderment is the ICRP's history of repeatedly lowering its guidelines for permissible dosage.

Between 1936 and 1958, the commission lowered its permissible annual doses four times: from 50 to 5 rem for the public, as distinct from industry workers. The 5-rem exposure standard was set according to a risk–benefit principle allowing a 1-in-5,000 chance of contracting cancer. The permitted dosage was further lowered in 1977 to 0.5 rem, and again in 1991 to 0.1 rem, following re-evaluation of cancer risk among atomic bomb survivors. The ICRP is now preparing to issue a new set of recommendations in 2005. As a senior British public health official once remarked, "There is something disturbing about the repeated assurances, 'This time, folks, we have got it right!'–when on each occasion, a previous understatement of hazard is revealed."

The more she read, the more incredulous Rosalie became about the "permissible" dose levels allowed. "I thought at first that I would be challenging the medical profession, and then I thought that I was taking on the nuclear power industry— but every time I tried to resolve the problem, I ended up back at the weapons industry."

Reflection, then Action

Dismayed by what she was learning about the hazards of the nuclear industry, and by what she saw as the lack of concern for public health on the part of political leaders and regulators, Rosalie decided to leave Roswell for a period of reflection. She announced this plan in a 1975 newspaper article on "Nuclear Suicide." After the article, an announcement appeared, displaying a characteristic blend of the practical and the spiritual in Rosalie's plans for the future. It was to be the first of many multi-stop speaking tours.

Available to speak. Sr. Rosalie Bertell is leaving her post as a biostatistician at Roswell Park Memorial Institute. She is deeply disturbed by the risks imposed by nuclear plants. She believes she will be "more fruitful" when she has made a change. She will be available to speak during an August tour stopping at Chicago, Omaha, Cheyenne, Salt Lake City, Reno, San Francisco, Los Angeles, Grand Canyon, Albuquerque, Oklahoma City, St. Louis, Pittsburgh, and Buffalo. She will be living in Barre, Vermont after September in prayerful reflection and probing of today's world and its values. For booking write Roswell Park Memorial Institute. Help defray the expense of her trip.

Speaking later about that period in her life, she observed, "I had to work it out within myself. I didn't know how to handle it .... During that retreat, I lost whatever internal resistance I had to being an activist. I think it takes a certain amount of contemplation before you can let down the barriers that keep you from doing things out of the ordinary."

She spent a year in Barre before she felt capable of accepting the task that seemed to await her. "I wanted to feel free enough to give myself to this work, to care nothing about money or status or what people think, or 'what a Sister ought to be doing' or what the bishop thought. I had to feel the earth suffering and I had to know that it didn't have to suffer .... No matter what anybody does, nobody can take my past away.

I've had a good life. But what will life hold for those now being born?"

Now in her late forties, she decided to "take on the whole thing."

CHAPTER 3

THE BIRTH OF THE "ANTI-NUCLEAR NUN"

Back in Buffalo after her year's absence, Rosalie resumed research at Roswell. She presented her research findings at professional meetings and joined her colleague Dr. Irwin Bross in criticizing widespread mammographic screenings. Rosalie pointed out a basic arithmetical error in the design of the New York Health Insurance screening program, which in her view could have resulted in serious health effects on early participants. "A lot of this I blame on the nuclear establishment, which has gone out of its way to convince everybody that low-level radiation is no hazard," she observed. "By letting nuclear physicists determine what doses of radiation were safe, the doctors have abdicated responsibility in this area." The line between the researcher and the activist was becoming increasingly blurred.

A speech she gave to a Quaker group in Burlington, Vermont, presents some of her basic themes during this period. She pointed to the public's "naïve trust" in an industry that had grown too quickly, without basic research on the safety problems and the impact of plant effluents on humans and the environment. She also revealed some of the ways in which nuclear defenders manipulated facts and figures about radiation dangers.

"We are told that effluents from a nuclear plant add to the environment only 1 percent of the radiation we naturally receive. Yet this [estimate] neglects to mention the qualitative difference between a plant's effluents and naturally occurring radionuclides .... Plutonium, which does not occur naturally, is the most deadly poison ever produced." Determined to expose the many ways in which statistics could be used to obscure uncomfortable realities in the nuclear debate, Rosalie pointed out the fallacy of averaging exposure estimates across the whole nation. This practice minimizes to the vanishing point the actual exposure levels to people in specific locations, and also ignores the fact that susceptibility to damage is not uniform.

Her supporters appreciated that she discussed radiation in plain language, rather than the arcane technical vocabulary often employed by the nuclear establishment. Her detractors, on the other hand, attacked her presentations as emotional, unscientific, and simplistic. Here is how she explained radioactivity and its dangers to a lay audience:

"When a material is radioactive, it means it periodically has an explosion on a microscopic level. Take, for example, just one atom of plutonium in a lung tissue. In exploding, it shoots out particles of energy through living cells. As you know, a cell is not empty, but a living system filled with different types of matter with separate jobs to do in the body. We cannot feel anything of this explosion on the cellular level. But it will do damage."

By 1976, Rosalie had begun the life-in-motion that was to characterize her existence until retirement—and after. Between 1976 and 1980, she travelled across North America and beyond, achieving a national reputation as "the anti-nuclear nun," following her visible success in helping to block the reactor construction at Lockwood. Rosalie became a sought-after "expert witness" in the public hearings necessary for nuclear plants to obtain a licence. Concerned citizens gradually learned to use the licensing system to delay construction and to have safety features added.

In Portland, Oregon, Rosalie appeared as a defence witness at the 1976 trial of 96 persons arrested for trespass during peaceful demonstrations at the nearby Trojan nuclear power plant. Following her testimony that long-term health dangers from routine low-level radiation had been seriously underestimated at Trojan, the jury voted to acquit all 96 on a technicality. "Afterwards," according to a local newspaper account, "jury members singled out Bertell's testimony as having most influenced them, despite the judge's instructions to ignore it." This nuclear plant, Oregon's first and only nuclear facility, closed in 1993 after a long history of serious problems. Many locals believe it was the inspiration for the accident-prone nuclear plant on the animated television series *The Simpsons*.

The trial of the so-called Limerick 14 in Pennsylvania also involved a non-violent protest at a nuclear plant construction site. In her affidavit, Rosalie highlighted a point that she repeated consistently across the years: the need for independent assessment and monitoring of the health status of people working in nuclear facilities or living nearby. It was not reasonable, she argued, that "people are being asked to trust the estimates of health effects generated by theoretical models with no verification or protection in legally viable documentation, and to welcome a self-monitoring nuclear power plant capable of destroying their health, their property, their financial stability, and their jobs."

Turning Point for Nuclear Power: The Clamshell Alliance

As anti-nuclear groups became involved in the licensing process and made contact with people like Rosalie, they learned more about the dangers and unsolved technical problems of nuclear energy. They also developed increasingly sophisticated tactics to delay reactor construction. In 1976, a movement began that by the end of the decade had helped to bring the nuclear industry to its knees. Despite the earlier prediction that 1,000 reactors would be operating by the turn of the century, as of 2003 there were only 103.

Rosalie participated from the beginning in the watershed events spearheaded by the Clamshell Alliance. The group was born following a proposal to construct twin nuclear power plants in Seabrook, New Hampshire. It brought together fishermen, clam diggers, and environmentalists, along with conservative New Englanders disturbed about a perceived threat to traditional seacoast life. A series of non-violent site demonstrations began in August 1976, attracting regional supporters and activists from across the United States and beyond. Fuelled by ongoing media attention, the 1977 demonstration drew 30,000 protesters, while the 1978 rally attracted more than 220,000, making it the largest anti-reactor protest in United States history. It touched off demonstrations across the country.

Rosalie was struck by the non-confrontational style of the Alliance, which she and others attributed to the presence of women in key leadership roles. The emphasis on consensus and non-violence contributed to the movement's conspicuous success. New Hampshire Governor Meldrim Thompson predicted outbreaks resulting from the "destructive doctrine of revolutionaries and communists." These rampages, perhaps disappointingly to the authorities, did not occur, but 1,400 protesters were arrested anyway.

Rosalie was one of the featured speakers at the rally. With

its references to the historic past and the traditional rights of American citizens, her address illustrated her knack of tailoring a message to suit her audience. "With you, I deeply regret the action of Governor Thompson to suppress opposition to nuclear power among state employees—a clear violation of free speech .... We are no less inflamed than our forebears and we refuse to be tyrannized by wealth or pseudo-learning .... We are a plain people, rooted in the earth and in real life, who match theory against reality." Shifting in her conclusion from past heritage to present hazard, she reminded her audience that the New England states were already among those with the highest cancer rates in the country.

In the subsequent trial of the protesters, Rosalie was the first expert witness for the defence. The week before she was to testify at Seabrook, her office was broken into and her testimony stolen. After scrambling to reproduce her statement, she was never allowed to deliver it. Following repeated interruptions by the attorney for the state, the judge ruled that anything she might have to say was irrelevant, and dismissed her. Helen Caldicott, medical doctor and expert in medical effects of radiation, was the next witness. She too was dismissed. Rosalie commented later that during the lunch hour, one of the reporters, a woman in her sixties, told her that she had been doing controversial stories for major newspapers all her adult life, "but had never seen anything like the paranoia which surrounds the question of radiation and health."

Despite the protests, construction continued at Seabrook, and one of the nuclear towers eventually became operational in 1990, after massive cost overruns. The second tower was never completed, and it was not until 2003 that dismantling of the empty hulk on the marshes began. Clamshell was also the catalyst for anti-nuclear protests across the country, bringing together Native American uranium miners, farmers, professionals, unions, housewives, activists, and religious groups. After the Seabrook protests, no new reactors were constructed in the United States, and 125 that were then in the process of construction or already opened were cancelled or closed. In the United States and Canada alike, growing popular disenchantment with nuclear power intensified the industry's search for new markets. The race was on to sell reactors to the developing world.

Making Waves, Making Headlines, Making Enemies

Increasingly, Rosalie encountered hostility at Roswell about her extracurricular nuclear activism. When she spoke and wrote now, she was careful to specify that she was not speaking for the Institute. But the media found that her forthright style of comment made good copy. For example, when Dr. Bernard Cohen, physicist at the University of Pittsburgh, commended the theory of hormesis—that a little bit of radiation was probably good for you, strengthening resistance in a manner similar to inoculation—Rosalie took public umbrage. "Referring to Dr. Bernard Cohen for advice on the medical effects of radiation, the economics of energy production, and on preserving American civilization has become ludicrous. It is like seeking the local bicycle repairman when you have appendicitis."

Some of her addresses were reprinted as magazine articles or pamphlets, and became important documents in the growing anti-nuclear movement. "Nuclear Power and Human Frailty," a speech delivered at an open meeting with the Ulster County Legislature and congressmen in New York state, denounced nuclear power as a colossal experiment on human beings. It was later reprinted and widely distributed by Syracuse Peace Council. "They've been going like hotcakes at the State Fair!" a friend wrote her. Her opponents dismissed these early speeches as exaggerated and hysterical. Years later, however, when classified material about nuclear accidents, dumping of nuclear wastes, and radiation experiments on human beings began to surface, Rosalie's words would come to be seen as understatements.

From the earliest days of her activist career, Rosalie took up the cudgels for groups that she saw as especially threatened by radiation: women and children; aboriginal, indigenous, and Third World peoples; workers in uranium mines and nuclear facilities. She saw these groups as doubly vulnerable in comparison to the white adult male professionals who ran the nuclear establishment and made the rules about "permissible" dose levels. The disadvantaged groups were more likely to receive excessive doses of radiation, and less likely to be able to mount an effective defence of their lives and health.

In one of her most popular early talks, "Nuclear Crossroads," she assailed the hazards to workers in nuclear weapons manufacturing. A special target of her criticism was the Rocky Flats Nuclear Weapons Plant near Denver, which produced plutonium triggers for all the nuclear bombs and missile warheads made in the United States. Its record of accidents, fires, and carelessness with radioactive wastes had finally touched off public demonstrations, despite official assurances that there was no cause for alarm. "There have been severe accidents at Rocky Flats and probably there is permanent contamination of the land, food and water. At least 381 workers have been exposed to radiation levels higher than permissible levels .... Will the people of Denver wait for government action to protect them from the raping of the land, the destruction of their life-supporting environment, the exploitation of their talents and labour, and the cruelest undermining of their life and health?" Later ranked as an environmental disaster and the worst facility in the entire nuclear arms production complex, Rocky Flats was finally shut down in the late 1980s.

Rosalie often conveyed her message about radiation effects

by telling stories based on her personal experiences. In 1979, at the invitation of the union, she visited the strike-bound Nuclear Fuel Services plant in Erwin, Tennessee. The sticking point in negotiations was the workers' demand for retirement at age 55, because they believed "they're not going to make it to 65." Rosalie was shocked at the men's appearance. "These were men who have worked 18 to 20 years making plutonium fuel rods for navy submarines," she recalls. "I met a man there 29 years old. I would've sworn he was 60. He had pure white hair. I spoke with about 100 men. Twelve of them have had spinal surgery for what the doctors are calling 'degenerative spine and premature aging.'"

All of the workers reported gross blood in their urine, which Rosalie saw as a sign that radioactive material was damaging delicate tissue in the kidneys or bladder. "The men were right," she said, "they're not going to make it to 65. The social pressures on them are great, because they're accused of being 'unpatriotic.' On the other hand, they can't get another job. No other employer wants to assume liability for a worker who has worked that long with radioactive materials."

On her return, she found herself repeatedly stonewalled in attempts to help the workers. A letter to the Director of Health Physics at the University of Rochester outlined what happened when she tried to set up blood tests to assess damage to bone marrow. "The men agreed, but the union doctors in Washington, D.C., failed to fulfill their function with respect to drawing blood and expressing it by air to Buffalo for analysis at Roswell."

Later, at a plant in New York state where Rosalie tried to do a worker follow-up, she encountered a series of stumbling blocks: legal blockades, a departmental reorganization, dissolution of the Environmental Health Section, and the firing of the official who had supported her study. Such events confirmed Rosalie's belief that the nuclear industry maintained its boast that "no damage to workers' health has ever been proven" by a simple expedient: preventing researchers from gathering information.

During this period, Rosalie had already begun research for what would become her comprehensive work on radiation hazards, *No Immediate Danger*, and there were few nuclear issues that escaped her scrutiny. In addition to speeches, she prepared affidavits, and the variety of topics she tackled indicates how extensively she was investigating both civilian and military aspects of nuclear energy.

In January 1979, she sent an affidavit to Honolulu about proposed naval weapons storage in Hawaii. She quotes from the Navy's environmental impact statement:

> In the event of a high explosive detonation, some pluto-
> nium material could be spread about the immediate area
> of the accident. This material will not cause radiological
> damage to personnel, regardless of one's proximity, if kept
> outside the body.

In her affidavit, she states that "there is no indication of the Navy's inability to retrieve this deadly material, no indication that the plutonium will eventually leave the immediate area of the accident or ... by entering into the water system and becoming airborne on dust particles, enter into human bodies. It is, in fact, impossible to keep the plutonium outside of the body once it is in the air, water, and food supply. Implying otherwise constitutes a cruel deception of the public with respect to a very potent carcinogen."

The Navy's statement goes on to advise that

> if plutonium is involved in a fire, radioactive particles will accompany the toxic gases in the smoke cloud. However, such smoke clouds are limited to the accident scene, quickly dissipate, and may constitute an internal hazard to personnel at the scene. The smoke should be avoided.

Later, Rosalie commented: "This is comparable to solving a drowning man's problems by telling him not to inhale water!"

Spreading Her Messages Abroad

Rosalie soon began to receive public-speaking requests from abroad. In May 1978, at the invitation of the Irish Transport and General Worker's Union, Rosalie travelled to the land of her maternal ancestors and spoke to workers in Dublin on "The Ethical Problems Involved in Nuclear Generation of Electricity." She was well aware of tensions that workers often experienced. They wanted jobs, but they did not wish to imperil their own health, or the health of their families and communities. The nuclear industry, for its part, did not hesitate to describe the anti-nuclear movement as a menace to employment and progress. In her address, Rosalie reconfigured the terms of the debate, placing it in the context of the history of the labour movement.

"The primary tension in this new industrial development is between the nuclear industry and the whole community, rather than between industry and labour. We have no means by which the community can enter the decision-making, and by which the community can be protected, as workers came to be protected by collective bargaining and workmen's compensation." Emerging community health problems demanded new responses. During the industrial age, the field of occupational health had emerged to deal with threats to workers' health and safety. In the nuclear age, the unfore-seen public health threats posed by radiation and other pollu-tants required a new discipline: environmental health.

Practical, down-to-earth, non-technical, her address shows her skill in communicating to an audience of working men. "Where, then, shall we go? How shall we find work and income and health for our families and for those who come after us? What options do we have?"

The energy choices she outlined were the ones she continued to support throughout her career, long before they became common currency: those based on renewable resources. "Technology," she said, "must be controlled by people and must contribute to human good." Such technologies include solar, wind, ocean hydro, bioconversion, geothermal, and fuel cell energies. Decentralized and relatively simple, Rosalie pointed out, these did not require elite technological experts to make all decisions and a security police to prevent violence, and they were ready to be used immediately on a small scale.

Rosalie's most moving experience as a speaker during this period occurred in August 1978 when she travelled to Osaka, her first of several trips to Japan. She felt honoured by an invitation to speak at the 33rd commemoration of the Hiroshima and Nagasaki bombings, sponsored by the Japanese International Congress Against Atomic and Hydrogen Bombs. In her address, she called for an international ban on radiation warfare, which she compared to the use of poison gas or bacteria: "all destroy the basic cellular life on which we depend for existence." This is also one of the early occasions when she explicitly called for the building of international structures, such as an effective World Court, to deal with problems that were international in scope.

The most profound and lasting impressions of the visit to Japan, however, related to the experience of staying at the home of a survivor of the bombing: listening to people's stories, understanding what had happened there 33 years before, resolving never to forget.

The "Atomic Veterans" and "Downwinders"

In the United States, too, there were survivors of the bombs. US troops had cleaned up in Japan, without being issued protective clothing or precautionary guidelines. From 1951 to 1957 at the Nevada test site, the military strove to produce "hardened" troops capable of "tactical" warfare on the atomic battlefield. Troops were ordered to observe nuclear tests and conduct "atomic war exercises" at or near ground zero immediately after the detonation. Moreover, from 1946 to 1963, both servicemen and residents who worked and lived "downwind" of the above-ground bomb tests in Nevada, Arizona, and Utah, were exposed to massive doses of radioactivity. No medical follow-ups were conducted by the Atomic Energy Commission, nor were warnings issued regarding potential health risks.

By the 1970s, the health damage suffered by US servicemen—those who had been exposed in Japan, at Pacific testing sites, and in the United States—had become evident. Among these "atomic veterans" was Lyman Quigley, who had participated in the Nagasaki cleanup. After years of suffering illnesses that the Department of Veterans' Affairs refused to acknowledge, Quigley tracked down 15 other men he had known in Nagasaki. Dispersed across the country, they were unaware of one another's post-war medical status. Nearly all had experienced agonizing health problems at an unusually early age: heart attacks, lung ailments, stomach pains, skin afflictions. None had received any service-connected benefits.

In the affidavit Rosalie provided to the State of Oregon, where Quigley was trying to have his health impairments recognized by the Veterans' Administration, she spoke about the duty to monitor the health of persons exposed to radioactive emissions: "Had the US military kept accurate health records of servicemen who cleaned up in Nagasaki, it would be possible to assign proportions of health effects to the exposure. In the face of governmental failure to do so, benefit of the doubt and compensation should be awarded the serviceman. This permanent pollution of the body of a service person, although it is a new type of military damage, has been acknowledged in the case of Agent Orange and should be acknowledged in the case of fission products."

Quigley was turned down again. He continued his research into the atomic veterans' cases until he died of his fifth heart attack the following year, at age 58.

For years, Rosalie championed the cases of atomic veterans and repeatedly testified on their behalf. Their claims were finally recognized when a landmark bill, the Radiation Exposed Veterans' Compensation Act of 1988, began to compensate atomic veterans suffering from 15 types of cancer linked to radiogenic damage. Two years later, another law, the Radiation Exposure Compensation Act of 1990, began providing benefits for civilians who had lived downwind of fallout from the Nevada tests, to uranium miners and millers, ore transporters, and participants at the Nevada test site.

One atomic veteran, a former navy flier, wrote her in 2003, describing an accident during nuclear testing 40 years earlier in the Pacific:

> On July 24, 1962, three aircrews and their ground support were caught on the ground when a Thor rocket with a 1.4-megaton warhead blew up on the pad. Plutonium was scattered all over the place when the safety officer destroyed the warhead to prevent a nuclear holocaust. It would be two days before the runway was cleared of debris and we could get our aircraft out of there.
>
> I'm telling you this because those airmen suffered an 85-percent casualty rate resultant from plutonium exposure. Twenty-five percent would experience reproductive inefficiency. My own wife and I would lose three children. Others would have similar experiences and would also suffer from a myriad of radiogenic diseases including non-Hodgkins lymphoma, multiple myeloma, thyroid cancer, kidney cancer, colon/rectal cancer, joint diseases, eyesight failure, spinal nerve damage, cancer of the esophagus ... to name a few ....

But you should know ... the many times you gave testimony before Congress led to legislation in our behalf, and many of the airmen, today, live because of you. That's a fact. I just wanted you to know that. We consider you the Angel on our shoulders.

The writer, Michael Thomas, subsequently became director of the Veterans' Rights Coalition and worked to get legislation passed to compensate affected veterans. He is now promoting a bill to benefit affected children of atomic veterans.

Proving the Hazards of Low-Level Radiation

The absence of monitoring for the atomic veterans and downwinders was only one aspect of the failure to record adequately the health status of those in contact with radiation and other forms of toxic pollution. Rosalie also became prominent at international forums demanding health monitoring across international boundaries. At a World Future Studies Conference in Berlin in 1979, she urged that technology be developed to monitor losses in human health, increased genetic load, and pollution of earth, air, and water. In a recommendation that showed that she was moving beyond a focus on the nuclear threat to other threats to life and habitat, she called for the creation of a Health Watch

International. Such an organization, she stated, could eventually become part of the existing World Health Organization (WHO), and could be empowered to monitor and report on all kinds of global pollution.

Despite the crusading efforts of people like Rosalie, the nuclear industry and its regulators continued to downplay the health hazards of radiation, and to dismiss the critics as uninformed, at best. Why has it been so difficult to "prove" conclusively that low doses of ionizing radiation harm people? Most people whose response to radiation has been studied, like atomic bomb survivors, have received doses of 100 rems or more. For many years, there was little reliable data for exposures of less than 10 rems, for people who live near nuclear power stations, or weapons factories, or waste dumps. In large part, this was because appropriate studies were rarely done—particularly the kinds of studies that could compare the health status of such people both before, and many years after, living with continued exposure to radiation.

The most frequently observed radiation effect is cancer. Yet radiation-induced cancers are indistinguishable from all other cancers and can only be detected statistically, in relation to the number of cancers that would normally be expected in a given population. Since industrial societies have high rates of cancer deaths, it may be statistically very difficult to detect a relatively small number of excess cancer deaths due to radiation.

Matters are also complicated by the need to continue a

study from the first exposure until death. With low-level exposures, a cancer may not appear for 30 or more years after it was induced, and study populations do not normally remain in place over decades. Moreover, choosing a comparison or "control" population to match the exposed group is difficult. For example, radiation workers are healthier at point of hiring than the general population, because they must pass rigorous physical exams to get the job. To take the "healthy worker effect" into account, then, the control group should also be healthier than the general population.

For such reasons, it has been difficult to carry out studies of low-level radiation exposure that would provide a more rational basis for "permissible doses" than the data on bomb victims. In the 1970s, however, such a study was published, by one of the top epidemiologists in the United States, Dr. Thomas Mancuso, and it rocked the regulatory and scientific establishment.

In 1965, the AEC asked Dr. Mancuso, a pioneer in the field of studying long-term health effects, to study the effects of radiation exposure on workers at the Hanford works in Washington state. Rosalie commented that the military considered Hanford "a showplace," because worker exposures there were lower than at other weapons plants. "It was the only one they allowed to be studied by independent scientists. Hence, Mancuso's eventual findings were very much resisted." This large nuclear weapons establishment, which dated back to the time of the Manhattan Project, included a plutonium reactor complex and a massive nuclear waste dump. Assembling data dating back to the mid-1940s, Mancuso proceeded to carry the study into the 1970s, in order to give long-latency cancers time to appear. At first he found no evidence that the workers suffered health damages greater than those of the general population.

Despite urgings from the AEC to publish progress reports showing these negative findings, he repeatedly refused to release his data prematurely. Confidential memos later obtained under the Freedom of Information Act confirmed what many had suspected. The AEC had commissioned the research for political reasons, notably the need to back up their unfailing, but never quite convincing assurances that employees were not suffering harmful effects. They also hoped that negative findings could be used to fight compensation claims for radiation-related injuries.

In 1974, Dr. Samuel Milham, another investigator, found an excess of cancers among Hanford workers in his study, which he presented to the AEC before publishing. The agency called Mancuso, dictating to him over the telephone the statement they wished him to make: that Milham's results were contrary to Mancuso's finding that there was *not* an excess of cancer deaths among Hanford workers. When Mancuso refused, he was informed that his contract, which had another year to run, would not be renewed after the expiry date.

In the last year of his contract, Mancuso recruited Alice

Stewart, the renowned British epidemiologist, and George Kneale, a statistician from England, to help him continue his data analysis. Their results confirmed that there were about 6 percent more deaths from certain types of cancers among Hanford workers than would normally be expected. Now that Mancuso was ready to publish, the AEC opposed publication, terminated his contract, seized his case files, and transferred the study to two other AEC facilities. However, Mancuso had kept a backup copy of his data, which he and his British colleagues proceeded to analyze and publish in a controversial paper, usually called the MSK Study. Subsequent re-analyses of the data have confirmed that among Hanford workers, there was a significant excess of multiple myeloma and cancer of the pancreas, both of which can be induced by radiation. Rosalie, who knew all of the participants well, expressed the admiration of a fellow mathematician for George Kneale's statistical analyses: "Exquisite!"

The Fate of "Rogue Scientists"

Mancuso was not the only scientist or health official who was quickly penalized when his findings countered the AEC "party line." Many others, some of them luminaries in the scientific world, also lost their reputations, their research grants, and their livelihood.

Back in the 1960s, Dr. Edward Weiss had noted an increase in leukemia deaths and thyroid cancers in southwestern Utah, an area downwind of radioactive fallout from nuclear testing. His federal funding was withdrawn. In a confidential memo, an AEC official outlined what was at stake: adverse public reaction, lawsuits, and jeopardy to programs at the Nevada test site.

Dr. John Gofman was one of the most highly respected scientists in the nuclear establishment. A brilliant nuclear chemist, he had, as a graduate student, discovered a way of separating plutonium from uranium, which had provided the Manhattan Project with the plutonium for its bombs. He later completed medical school, and taught molecular cell biology at the University of California at Berkeley. He was then appointed director of radiobiological studies at the AEC Lawrence Livermore Laboratory in Northern California, an important nuclear complex overseen by the AEC.

By 1969, he and his colleague, Dr. Arthur Tamplin, had concluded there was no basis for the AEC's claim that there was a safe threshold of radiation. They estimated that the cancer risk from radiation was about 20 times greater than previously thought, and that the hazard to future generations in the form of genetic damage had been underestimated even more seriously. Their staff and budget were slashed. Gofman and Tamplin subsequently resigned. They co-authored *Poisoned Power*, a manifesto against the nuclear energy option published in 1971, and began appearing at public debates, hearings, and anti-nuclear rallies. Their strong scientific credentials conferred considerable credibility on the gathering protest movement against nuclear energy.

Dr. Carl Johnson, health director in the Colorado county where the Rocky Flats plutonium plant is located, was asked to approve a routine expansion of residential zoning adjacent to the plant. His analyses of soil samples revealed plutonium concentrations more than 3,000 times higher than normal in some cases. Further investigation found increases in many types of cancer for persons living in exposed areas. Dr. Johnson was fired.

There were many others. At the 1978 US congressional hearings on behalf of Mancuso and Stewart, Dr. Irwin Bross characterized attempts to suppress the MSK Study findings, and those of the Tri-State Leukemia Study, as part of "a sordid story extending back to the furor over fallout from weapons testing. It is a story where researchers were rewarded for not finding any hazards and punished if they failed to support the official AEC line that these low levels of radiation are harmless."

The Tri-State researchers, including Rosalie, would be the next to go.

CHAPTER 4

THE YEARS OF LIVING DANGEROUSLY

The Tri-State Survey's research grant from the National Cancer Institute came up for renewal in 1978. The outcome was not a surprise. The Survey's results linking X-rays to leukemia, the criticism of mammography screening, and Rosalie's outspoken anti-nuclear activism had ruffled the radiological profession, the nuclear industry, and her employers at Roswell Park. The National Cancer Institute withdrew the team's funding, appending a note to the bottom of the grant proposal. "If you would like to change your line of research, you could submit a new request for funds. We would be very happy to consider it." Rosalie characterized this suggestion as outrageous and resigned on June 1, 1978. The research team, down to nine people, dispersed.

Axing the Tri-State Survey strengthened the growing perception of high-level political interference in radiation matters. In a letter to the secretary of the Department of Energy (DOE), Senator John Durkin expressed concern "that actions by your department appear to have had the effect of discouraging research into the health effects of low-level radiation." Expressing dismay at "the pattern of DOE interference with these essential independent studies," he went on: "Dr. Bertell's funding was recently cut off by the National Cancer Institute after unsigned critiques of her work were circulated, apparently by Dr. James Liverman, the acting assistant secretary for environment at DOE. Dr. Liverman did not see fit to send copies of the critiques to Dr. Bertell, although they challenge her professional competence."

Increasing public awareness of problems at the DOE would eventually lead to a major shakeup in the nuclear establishment, but not in time to save Rosalie's academic career. At the age of 49, she forfeited all the perquisites of her research appointment, including her academic connection with the School of Graduate Studies at the State University of New York. Years later she described her sense of loss at "having no typist or support staff, no photocopier or printing department, no prestigious affiliation or scientific colleagues with whom to share ideas and research findings." She never regained a foothold in academia.

The Ministry of Concern for Public Health (MCPH)

However, since the handwriting on the wall had long been visible, Rosalie regrouped quickly. Her creation of the

Ministry of Concern for Public Health (MCPH) illustrates that blend of the practical and the visionary that characterized her life and work. In July, she wrote to the Grey Nuns Council asking for their permission "to devote my time and energy to a Ministry of Concern for Public Health," which would focus on radiation damages sustained by the public as a result of nuclear enterprises. "I expect to do this in collaboration with GEA [Global Education Associates]. For the present, I would be working with them from my Buffalo office, sharing insights and hopes." She provided the names of her legal advisers, and her plans for setting up appropriate financial arrangements. Mindful that reverses were possible, she concluded: "I would certainly try not to be caught without funds, and somehow feel that the backing, both earthly and heavenly, will prevent such a situation."

By September 1978, the MCPH was in place. In her letter to the Grey Nuns, she listed her fee structure and other sources of support as follows: expert witness, $400; lectures (college/hospital) $100; consultant $150 per day; travel costs to be covered by the sponsoring group; begging; and divine providence. Moreover, she hoped that Audrey Mang, a skilful writer who had agreed to help her with secretarial work, would "popularize some of my findings, and we can split the commission on the publications."

One of the individuals who congratulated her on setting up the MCPH was Karl Morgan. He was the founder of

health physics, an academic specialty that evolved during the Manhattan Project years. It aims to recognize, evaluate and control all health hazards from ionizing radiation. Chairman for 14 years of the ICRP's committee on internal dose, Morgan became a scientific pariah in the mid-1970s when he said that the permissible dose should be halved. "Unfortunately," he wrote, "most scientists, medical doctors, and lawyers have put their jobs before what they know to be the truth in many cases. I am especially proud of persons of stature like yourself that are willing to go all out to defend the community against the powerful organization that gets what it wants the way it wants it only because money talks. It is people like you that make democracy work."

The following year Rosalie formalized her agreement with Global Education Associates, a peace education organization with which she had long-established ties of co-operation and friendship. GEA had a strong base in religious communities and a global reach. They agreed to accept Rosalie's initiative as an international task force dealing with health and energy issues, under their auspices. This gave the MCPH both non-profit corporation status and non-governmental organization status at the United Nations. Apart from creating an organizational framework for her own activities, Rosalie hoped to lend professional support to individual researchers. "We have no vested interests, and even stand to lose funding and reputation because of our determination to protect the public health rather than military and economic policy."

Drawing on the business sense she had assimilated as her father's daughter, Rosalie kept detailed records of the expenses, income, and work of the MCPH, which in effect was *her* work. A 1982 tally of her major activities from 1979 to 1982 is an eye-opener: research projects in the United States, Canada, West Germany, and the United Kingdom; research plans for the Marshall Islands, French Polynesia, and the United States; the publication of *Handbook for Radiation Health Effects*. She gave lectures or workshops to 74 religious groups, 68 colleges, 119 public or citizens' groups, and 69 hospitals or health workers' groups. There were 83 such events in 1979, 79 in 1980, 66 in 1981, and 83 in 1982. Thus, touching down on four continents, she averaged almost 80 engagements annually during those four years.

This is a remarkable record of activity. Rosalie was in her fifties and her health was not robust. She was always financially strapped, and much of the administrative and promotional effort behind the crowded agenda fell on her shoulders. In addition to far-flung speaking engagements during this period, she also continued research on *No Immediate Danger*, worked on professional publications, and moved to a new country. It is not surprising that she wrote in 1980, en route from Australia to India, "I'm tired! This is a lonely life—I could use a day of quiet and silence. Perhaps soon!"

At the time Rosalie set up the MCPH, the civilian nuclear power industry in the United States was struggling to survive. In December 1978, she was invited to speak about the nearby Robert E. Ginna nuclear power plant on a popular 6 p.m. news program in Rochester. When the utility company heard of the proposal, they demanded equal time and dispatched a trio of representatives: a vice-president, a public relations specialist, and a health physicist who was the designated spokesman.

There was a brief debate between Rosalie and the rather inarticulate young physicist, whose performance clearly displeased his escorts. One of them followed Rosalie as she departed. "As I went out the door, he shook his fist at me and said, 'We'll get you! Stay out of here and never come back to Rochester. We don't want you here.'" Rosalie considered reporting the threat to the police, but decided to leave and calm herself down before delivering a speech that evening. Two newspaper clippings that Rosalie saved from this period suggest that local nuclear facilities may have been especially sensitive to public criticism because of increased government surveillance, and the onset of costly damage claims. One story notes that the Robert E. Ginna plant was among the 33 Westinghouse-designed plants that the Nuclear Regulatory Commission had ordered temporarily shut down because of possible cracks in pipes. A spokesman for the utility denied that the condition represented a significant hazard. The other clipping reported that three lawsuits charging undue radiation exposure were pending against Rochester Gas and Electric Corporation.

By this time, even federal government offices were complaining that radiation policies were inadequate and dangerous. The US Government Accounting Office, for example, warned that official radiation monitoring did not even measure exposure for 40 percent of the population and provided only an "educated guess" regarding the exposure level of the remaining 60 percent. They added that "levels of radiation are increasing and affect not only the health of current populations, but of future generations because of genetic damage." In 1979, another government study reported that areas around nuclear facilities should be better prepared for nuclear emergencies.

By chance, this report was released two days after the nuclear accident at Three Mile Island.

Three Mile Island

On March 28, 1979, a succession of mistakes, malfunctions, and misinterpretations at the Three Mile Island (TMI) nuclear plant near Harrisburg, Pennsylvania, brought the facility to within a half hour of meltdown. The most serious nuclear accident in US history, TMI spewed radioactive effluents over the countryside, and drove a stake through the heart of the US nuclear power industry. Reassuring press releases compared maximum exposures to a single X-ray, and a massive public relations campaign by government and regulators swung into gear, downplaying the event. Dr. Edward Teller, an architect of the Manhattan Project, later claimed that the only injury caused by the explosion was the heart attack he experienced as a result of the uproar. Dr. Teller died at age 95 in 2003.

A citizens' health survey of 300 people living downwind gathered many reports of injuries and deaths among pets and livestock. In the succeeding months, investigators condemned careless procedures by operating personnel, and lax training by Metropolitan Edison. The Nuclear Regulatory Commission was criticized for its low standards of worker performance and inadequate response to the accident. Research was done to examine the psychological effects of "stress" surrounding the accident, but not its physical effects on humans and animals.

A story that Rosalie told later illustrates the kinds of tactics used to conceal the effects of the explosion. "The most ridiculous piece of science I've ever seen happened after Three Mile Island. A man raised birds commercially and in one afternoon during the accident, he lost about 1,400 birds. He connected this event with the accident, called the local health department, which called Washington. In no time, officials came to his house and went off with those dead birds. I saw the paper he received from the US Department of Agriculture. It was a form list of known bird diseases, every one of which had been checked 'no.' In the space at the bottom of the page, it said 'No known cause.' And that's what he got back in the middle of the TMI accident, with 1,400 birds killed in one afternoon. 'Nuclear fission accident' was not on the government's list!"

By chance, *The China Syndrome*, a thriller starring Jane Fonda as an intrepid reporter investigating a massive cover-up at a nuclear plant, had been released just three weeks earlier. In the course of the film, Fonda interviewed a safety expert who told her that a meltdown could "force the evacuation of an area the size of Pennsylvania." The film played to packed audiences nationwide.

The TMI accident touched off a wave of anti-nuclear protests in the United States and Europe, culminating in a monster peace rally in New York City in 1982 that attracted 1.3 million people. In 1981, citizens' groups won a class-action suit against the Three Mile Island facility, and an out-of-court settlement of $15 million, with a provision that part of the money be used to study the health effects of low-level ionizing radiation. Scientists continue to debate the long-term health effects on humans of TMI.

Critics and Enemies

Another corporation offended by Rosalie's continuing critiques and high-profile public image was Consolidated Edison (CE), a major player in the nuclear power industry. In September 1979, Dr. H.E. Bliss of CE's Chicago office asked for an opinion of Rosalie's scientific credentials from John H. Rust, professor emeritus of Radiology at the University of Chicago. The expansive reply illustrates some of the strategies used by her opponents to discredit her. The tone is patronizing. Rosalie is never referred to by her academic title, but always as "Sister." Her understanding of biology, her knowledge of past research, and her authority to speak on radiation issues are all dismissed. "With so many people, like Sister Rosalie Bertell," Dr. Rust begins, "there is a keen and deep-felt desire to give greater protection to people from the unseen and the unrecognized hazards of life." He concedes that she is capable in biometrics, but there is nothing new about her work on radiation aging. She overlooks the complexity of biological systems, and fails to deal adequately with the issue of low-level exposure over a long period of time. "In summary, I must conclude that this is another effort to use simple mathematics in an unsuitable manner to establish a point that was possibly well-established in the operator's mind before the study was started .... I return to my original position that she did it for humanistic reasons. For that she can be forgiven."

This letter was "leaked" to the press, and passed on to Rosalie by an ally in the media. She quickly dispatched a copy of the letter, along with a message of her own, to Robert Minogue at the Nuclear Regulatory Commission (NRC). Her reply illustrates both her prompt and assertive style of self-defence and her ability to forge useful alliances and a network of support.

"The enclosed letter," she writes, "was given me last week by a media person who had been pressured to refuse me normal coverage. I was there on the invitation of the citizen group and the mayor of Mexico, New York, to speak on low-level radiation. It is clear that generating this letter was Consolidated Edison's response to my petition for an NRC adjudicatory hearing on worker health." Noting that it would take a long time to deal with "such gross errors," she concluded that the writer seemingly had failed even to read her work. "What should I do about this kind of shafting from ambush?" she asks. "How can we get the scientific questions into a formal hearing and properly handled?"

On the same day, she wrote a brief note to Dr. Rust. "Dear Mr. Rust: The enclosed poorly written critique of my work was being circulated to members of the media in Oswego, New York, last week in an attempt to undermine my credibility. The astute reader familiar with my work would not be impressed, but the uninitiated might. Please inform me within 10 days whether or not the letter was written by you, and whether or not you authorized Consolidated Edison to use it in this unprofessional way. Thank you."

A telegram arrived within the allotted time. "Yours of 28 received 5 October. The letter in question was written by me at the request of Dr. Bliss. No restrictions were placed upon its use since it was a personal communication. I have not nor has anyone at Consolidated Edison given permission for its public distribution."

During the same period, an attempt was made to exert pressure on her through the Catholic Church. Following an address Rosalie gave to the College of St. Rose, Dr. John Matuszek, Director of New York State Radiological Sciences Laboratory, protested to the Most Reverend Howard J. Hubbard, Bishop of Albany. In his letter, Matuszek defended nuclear power, flayed Rosalie's research, and criticized the stance of the Diocese in appearing to countenance her temerity. "You should be aware," he wrote, "that Sr. Bertell and her mentor, Dr. Irwin J. Bross, have in the past presented their concepts to scientific peers, to Congressional committees and to various regulatory authorities. In every case, the concepts have been deemed inaccurate or unsubstantiated ... [and found] not acceptable for publication in scientific journals. As a result, Sr. Bertell and Dr. Bross have turned to publishing in the lay press, where scientific validity need not be proven, or to politicized presentations such as the seminar at St. Rose. For the Diocese to lend its support to such a presentation is to me unconscionable."

The bishop passed this missive on to Rosalie, who responded without delay. Beginning with an expression of regret "that someone in his position feels impelled to disseminate such vague, intangible, and damaging insinuations without accountability," Rosalie went on to address Dr. Matuszek's charges that her work and that of Dr. Bross had not been published by reputable journals, and that she had been reduced to writing for the lay press.

> Dr. Bross's work has been accepted in the *New England Journal of Medicine* and the *Journal of the American Public Health Association*. My methodology has been published in the *Journal of Surgical Oncology* and in two international journals, the *Journal of Medicine* and *Experientia*. I have presented my methodology at the international meeting of the Biometric Society without controversy. I have published,

and will continue to publish, in the lay press as well as in scientific journals. Since it is ultimately the American people who pay for scientific research, I feel an obligation to inform them of findings. This is especially necessary in the area of radiation-related research, where vested interests have a large stake in information control .... Thank you for your openness in sharing both this letter and your concern for the Church's position on the nuclear issue.

"Who Is Trying to Kill Sister Rosalie?"

Soon after this exchange, an attempt was made on Rosalie's life. She was not the first nuclear critic whose outspokenness placed her life in jeopardy. Numerous suspicious accidents and deaths had been whispered about over the years. The most celebrated target had been Karen Silkwood, a young technician at Kerr-McGee, the plutonium processing plant in Oklahoma. Having become increasingly apprehensive about working conditions at the plant, Silkwood finally informed AEC officials in Washington that Kerr-McGee was violating health and safety regulations. Her story was later dramatized in the 1983 film *Silkwood*, starring Meryl Streep as the doomed whistle-blower.

On November 13, 1974, Silkwood's car went off the road as she was driving to meet a labour union official and a *New*

York Times reporter with evidence supporting her allegations. The Oklahoma highway patrol ruled that the fatal accident was caused by her falling asleep at the wheel, though later investigations by a private detective found signs that the car had been pushed from behind. The documents she had been carrying were never found. Following the efforts of two determined young women activists, Silkwood's father filed a claim for damages against Kerr-McGee.

The Silkwood case had been much in the news during 1979. It finally came to trial in March, during the same month in which the Three Mile Island accident had placed nuclear issues in the headlines. In a landmark decision, a federal jury found against Kerr-McGee, awarding heavy damages to Karen Silkwood's estate.

About six months later, Rosalie experienced what seemed for a few terrifying minutes a replay of the Silkwood scenario. In October of that year, Rosalie delivered a talk on radiation dangers, widely publicized in advance, at the Highland Hospital in Rochester, the city from which she had been "banished" by the nuclear executive a year before.

Driving home afterwards in rush-hour traffic, she was in the middle lane of a highway three lanes wide when suddenly, "I became conscious of a white car in the left lane. It was too close to my car, so I pulled back, and when I did, the driver manoeuvred into my lane directly in front of me and dropped a very heavy sharp object—metal, I think—out of the car, in line with my front left tire. I saw it coming, but I couldn't move out of the way. I tried to straddle it, but it caught the inside of the tire and totally blew it. I think if I had hit it head-on, it could have turned the car over because I was in a small Toyota."

While she was examining the damage, a brown car marked "Sheriff" pulled over. There were two people in the car, and she didn't see the driver; the passenger was not wearing a uniform. "[The passenger] asked what happened and, when I told him, he wanted to know if I had either the licence number of the car or the piece of metal itself. I said 'No' to both questions. Then he told me that this wasn't their jurisdiction, but they had radioed the local Rochester police who would be there any minute. "

The police never came. Now mistrustful of the highway, she made her way home on back roads, and contacted her lawyer brother, who visited the sheriff's office the next morning. The police verified that the second car had not been a sheriff's car. "The second car," Rosalie concluded, "apparently was connected to the first one and had followed to see what had happened." In discussing the incident afterwards, she emphasized that she had no proof that the previous threat was related to her mysterious accident. Clearly, however, someone wanted her out of the way.

The event brought newspaper headlines, feature stories in magazines ("Who is trying to kill Sister Rosalie?"), and an outpouring of sympathy and support. Newpaper articles recounted past attempts at censorship and loss of research funding. Serious concerns now assailed Rosalie about whether the United States was a safe place for her particular brand of science and activism. Temporarily, however, she set them aside, as she headed off on her first visit to a new continent.

The Reception Down Under

Threats and harassment did not prevent her from making a long-planned trip to Australia, under trade union sponsorship. For a month, she visited all the Australian states, addressing workshop meetings, health professionals, church groups, and well-attended public rallies. Drawing on her experiences in the United States, she set about alerting trade union members and the public to the long-term hazards of uranium mining, nuclear reactors, and radioactive wastes left over from mining and milling.

She also testified before the Select Committee on Uranium Resources of the Australian legislature in Adelaide, observing that uranium miners are exposed to radiation hazards both through airborne particles and by inhaling radon gas. She informed them that the grandchildren of uranium miners in New Mexico were suffering from bone cancer, thus demonstrating the genetic effects of radiation that had been known since Dr. Hermann Muller won the Nobel Prize for his work in that area.

Turning to her recent experiences in Australia, she continued, "I was able to go to the tailings dump [uranium mining wastes] in Rum Jungle. It is not behind a fence and there is no warning on radioactivity. The dump is higher than the piles in the US, and unguarded. There was a sign that the water from the water supply was not fit to drink, but I did not notice birds and animals reading the sign."

While she received a courteous reception from the Legislative Council, the nuclear establishment did not invite her to speak with them on a professional level, nor did it respond to her invitation to a public debate. In Sydney, she was interviewed on a radio talk show. "During the interview," she wrote later, "one of Australia's 'reliable experts,' hidden in another room at the radio studio and listening to the interview, kept sending written messages to the interviewer. After I left the studio, the 'responsible expert' was allowed 15 minutes air time to denounce what I had said, without rebuttal. He attacked my competence and personal integrity. I was denied time to respond to the direct slander .... I will have my lawyer brother write to him when I get home." Further slights appeared in a letter published by the *Medical Journal of Australia*. The writer stated there was no scientific evidence supporting Rosalie's views, and added: "Sr. Bertell's addresses are aimed at the emotions and she seeks sympathy by listing the crimes, ranging from suppression of the facts to attempted murder, of those who oppose her opinions."

Nevertheless, she rejoiced at her reception from the union members who had invited her and the public who flocked to hear her speak. "I have warm memories of Australia," she says. "Several union members expressed the opinion that it was the most successful and important 'foreign visit' they had ever sponsored." The State Council (Unions) in Melbourne honoured her with a standing ovation—only the third ever given and the only one to a woman.

Following this trip and another to India, Rosalie was faced with an opportunity, and a decision. The Jesuit Centre for Social Faith and Justice, located in Toronto, Canada, had asked her to join them in their work, as a specialist in energy and public health. Briefly, she hesitated. Buffalo was home— yet home no longer seemed a comfortable place. Perhaps it was time to take up the maternal half of her heritage. Rosalie headed north.

CHAPTER 5

A TIME TO BLOOM

In the last chapter of *No Immediate Danger*, "A Time to Bloom," Rosalie turns to hopeful possibilities for the future. It also seems an appropriate caption for the decade that witnessed the blossoming of her career in Toronto. She created a public health institute there, won an international reputation as spokesperson on health and environmental issues, and garnered an array of honorary degrees and awards that signalled recognition in her adopted country and beyond.

Professionally, Canada was not an unknown country to Rosalie when she arrived in 1980. She had testified on the hazards of uranium mining and refining at inquiries in British Columbia, Saskatchewan, and Ontario. By comparison with the American nuclear scene, the one north of the border had much that appealed to Rosalie: a high level of nuclear awareness among British Columbia activists, who had successfully resisted uranium mining in their province; physicians with enlightened attitudes towards radioactive health threats. Above all, there was Canada's choice not to make nuclear weapons. "I chose to live in Canada," she wrote in her 2001 acceptance speech for the MacBride Peace Prize, "because of a long distaste for the US superpower mentality and constant escalation of the nuclear arms race. It was difficult to plan and work creatively for a peaceful and free world while constantly having to respond to the 'next generation' of weaponry."

Correspondence between a nuclear official and an activist nun in Saskatchewan indicates that supporters and opponents were in place as Rosalie crossed the border. "A couple of weeks ago in a telephone conversation," wrote an official from Eldorado Nuclear to Sister Teresita Kambeitz early in 1980, "I undertook to find out for you something about the submission made by Sr. Rosalie Bertell during the hearing

on Eldorado's proposal to build a refinery in the Port Granby area of Ontario. [It was] her usual anti-nuclear statement, which she has presented on many occasions. In fact, it appears that she has done a minimum of original work. An independent evaluation of that study found the conclusions to be without basis and the study to be almost worthless."

But Sister Teresita then corresponded with Rosalie, acknowledging the inspiration she had received from Rosalie's work. "Greetings from sunny Saskatchewan!" she wrote. "I thought you might be interested to hear a little about the hearings regarding the [uranium] refinery to be built at Warman. Over 200 oral briefs were given, the vast majority being in opposition to the refinery .... I am enclosing a letter which I thought you might 'enjoy.'... God bless you and your ministry."

These kinds of reactions to her anti-nuclear message might be familiar to Rosalie, but she still faced the uncertainties of carving out a niche for herself in a country with a different nuclear history from that of the United States.

Atoms for Canada

Canada began its nuclear journey during the Second World War when uranium from Canada and the Congo was used to produce the world's first atomic bombs. Due to its abundant reserves of uranium and strategic location, Canada became a junior partner with the United States and Britain in the Manhattan Project. In 1943, a joint Canadian–UK team was established in Montreal to develop nuclear reactors using heavy water. Having manoeuvred through the secrecy, mistrust, and rivalries of the war years, Canada had accumulated enough experience and technological know-how by the time the war was over, to develop its own independent nuclear program.

In the summer of 1944, Chalk River, Ontario, was chosen as the site of Canada's first heavy water test reactor, and by September 1945—a month after the war ended—the facility was up and running. Two further research reactors were established there, and Atomic Energy of Canada Limited (AECL) was formed as a Crown corporation of the federal government. AECL was charged with developing nuclear energy for peaceful purposes only, and the Atomic Energy Control Board (AECB) became the official regulatory body. With strong leadership from the federal government and the scientific community, and massive support from the Canadian taxpayer, Canada's unique nuclear reactor, the CANDU (Canadian Deuterium Uranium reactor), developed rapidly.

Hailed as a triumph of contemporary Canadian technology, CANDU appeared to hold out many commercial benefits: unlimited domestic energy from nuclear plants, international reactor sales, uranium exports, abundant capital investment. Pursuing nuclear technology would also help to guarantee the growth of a technologically advanced Canadian industry, and stimulate high-level research, training, and industrial development. Yet the potential dangers of the new technology were revealed early on. A violent nuclear accident in 1952 destroyed the core of the Chalk River NRX research reactor. Hundreds of American and Canadian military men were brought in to help with the radioactive cleanup operation, including Jimmy Carter, future US president.

In 1962, Canada's first nuclear power plant was opened at Rolphton, Ontario. This was followed by a larger prototype, now the Bruce Nuclear Power site, located on the Bruce Peninsula, which juts out between Georgian Bay and Lake Huron, northwest of Toronto. The initial operating success of these reactors indicated that the heavy water CANDU design was a viable technology. These reactors were followed quickly in the 1970s by Ontario Hydro's larger-scale stations: Bruce A on the Bruce Peninsula, and Pickering A, located on the eastern outskirts of Toronto on the shores of Lake Ontario. In marketing CANDU reactors abroad, AECL stipulated that they must be used for civilian nuclear energy production only. The hope was that CANDU would enable not only Canadians, but people in developing countries to enjoy the benefits of electricity at low costs. In the late 1950s, India and Pakistan became the first nations outside of Canada to install CANDU-type reactors.

Setbacks in the Seventies

In the decade before Rosalie arrived in Canada, however, the nuclear industry, which had begun with such high hopes, began to face unanticipated problems.

In 1974, India exploded its first atomic bomb, using weapons-grade plutonium produced in its Canadian-supplied reactor. Canada suspended nuclear co-operation with India pending negotiations. While India protested that its nuclear device was a "peaceful nuclear explosive," it was becoming clear that Canada had no effective recourse against countries that chose to ignore their commitment not to produce weapons. As time passed, a pattern emerged of bribes, corruption, and financial losses in the sales—or attempted sales—of CANDU reactors abroad. Moreover, the states seeking reactors all seemed to be authoritarian regimes—Argentina, South Korea, Romania—more intent on enhancing their political power and prestige than on providing cheap electricity to their impoverished citizens.

At home, also, the difficulty of circumventing the nuclear arms embrace was evident, as Canada became increasingly involved with American nuclear weapons production and deployment. Canadian policy-makers agreed to plans for testing the American cruise missile in Western Canada; to the manufacture of cruise missile parts at Litton Systems north of Toronto; and to US nuclear submarines being stationed in British Columbia coastal waters. All these initiatives, which to many seemed in clear violation of Canada's "peaceful atom" policy, fanned protests from coast to coast.

On the domestic energy front, the economic rationality of the nuclear option also came in for increasing challenge. Lessened demand for electricity and heightened awareness of nuclear hazards had cooled the demand for nuclear reactors. Despite public opposition, AECL went ahead with a new reactor in New Brunswick in 1975. The eventual cost of Pointe Lepreau was triple the original estimate, and the reactor was not operational until eight years later, in 1983. By that time, the province had an electric power surplus, and resorted to selling its excess power cheaply to New England. The outcome was not lost on the public: larger debt for New Brunswick taxpayers, and higher profits for American utilities companies.

Nothing, however, caused more alarm than growing awareness of the hazards posed by nuclear wastes. This issue was dramatized with the revelation in 1976 of radioactive dumping by Eldorado Mines in Ontario. Eldorado had dumped 200,000 tons of radioactive waste all over Port Hope, Ontario, until the mid-1960s. Radioactive waste had been used as landfill for two schools and more than 100 other sites where radiation levels were unacceptable. AECB ordered an investigation and cleanup.

Yet despite public outcry, AECB approved El Dorado's plans to expand their uranium refinery in 1979. No provisions were included for waste disposal, nor for the study of health effects, despite the fact that doctors had already reported an unusually high incidence of cancer in the district. Astonishingly, one AECB official remarked that such follow-up research was unnecessary "because the effects are supposed to take 10 to 20 years to appear."

It was on such scenes of mounting troubles that Rosalie appeared.

Moving In and Moving Out

When she first moved to Toronto, Rosalie took up residence at the Jesuit Centre on Dufferin Road and immediately began making contacts and forming judgments. A journal entry for November 7 notes

> Yesterday was a hectic day. In the morning we had a press conference to announce my presence at the Jesuit Centre …. There was a debate in the evening sponsored by the Canadian Environmental Law Association. Sternglass [Ernest Sternglass, prominent American anti-nuclear scientist] came and was very good. Dr. X of Chalk River was arrogant and lacking in scientific integrity. Y of the Atomic Energy Board was incredibly ignorant! The audience was visibly moved by the irrationality of the whole nuclear establishment.

Fears for her security arose that month, when three troubling incidents occurred a few weeks apart. First, an intruder entered the Jesuit Centre building, an event excitedly reported by a children's group meeting in the basement. Since there was no sign of unauthorized entry, the police simply reported an "occurrence." Two weeks later, in the early hours of the morning, there was a break-in. Nothing was missing, and the broken window was attributed to "childish malice." Shortly afterwards, a shooting occurred, producing two holes in one window and one in another, all converging on a pigeon coop, according to the police. The detectives showed Rosalie two BB pellets, ascribed the shooting to a running battle between pigeon fanciers and pigeon haters in the neighbourhood, and concluded that the three events did not constitute a pattern of conspiracy or harassment. They were unable to explain a 22-calibre bullet found at the scene by a priest. Quite possibly these events were random occurrences, but they were bound to be unsettling for someone who had just left her American home because she feared for her physical safety.

Rosalie resumed the pattern of activities that she had established in Buffalo: public speaking, consulting, research, and writing. By this time, her work was beginning to win public recognition. Shortly after leaving the United States, in the spring of 1981, she had received awards from the National Organization of Women (NOW), and from the New York

Public Interest Group. Two European awards followed in 1983, both recognizing her contributions in the field of human health.

By late 1983, she was hoping to launch a Canadian-based institute to advance her work. A letter written in December of that year announces, "I have resigned from the Jesuit Centre, and am discerning whether to stay in Canada or return to Buffalo." Six months later, the plans were in place. Together with Dr. Ursula Franklin, a well-known physicist and peace activist at the University of Toronto, and Dr. Dermot McLoughlin, a medical radiologist, Rosalie founded the International Institute of Concern for Public Health (IICPH). It would provide scientific and technical assistance on environmental hazards to government agencies, citizens' groups, labour unions, and indigenous and Third World peoples. It is noteworthy that the focus had expanded from the hazards of nuclear radiation to "environmental hazards." The Institute soon announced plans to publish a journal, *International Perspectives in Public Health*, with Rosalie as Editor-in-Chief.

Radiation Victims I: First Nations Peoples

Ever since she had first become aware of the plight of Native-American uranium miners in the American southwest, and of aboriginal miners in Australia, Rosalie had been outraged by the many ways in which Native and Third World peoples had been damaged by modern technology and industry, usually without their informed consent. The first country to mine uranium on a large scale, Canada had developed during the war years a network of mines, processing plants, and transportation that made it a leading exporter of uranium for atomic bombs. Most mineworkers were aboriginal peoples from Ontario, Saskatchewan, and the Northwest Territories.

Rosalie made many arduous trips to work with Native peoples in northern uranium mining communities, disaster zones where tons of radioactive mine tailings scar the landscape. These are the leftover piles of radioactive sand remaining after the rocks containing uranium are brought to the surface and crushed. Often in her subsequent talks, Rosalie showed slides of these trips and the mountains of tailings. "This is the beautiful Canadian North. If you look down from an airplane you see the ground looking like this. This is not snow. Now when it was under the ground in rock form it really was not that hazardous. It's now crushed so it's much more bioavailable." As she explained, if the radioactive sand is left on the surface and allowed to dry out, it can blow in the winds, land on distant vegetation, enter the food chain, and contaminate distant rivers and lakes.

The mineworkers and their communities were exposed to multiple radiation hazards: working in the mines without protective equipment, living near piles of radioactive waste, and being exposed to airborne and waterborne radioactive pollution. During the course of her work in the North, Rosalie created a comprehensive Community Health Survey, which she was later to adapt and use for assessing local health in communities in the developing world.

She first used the Survey with Native bands living on the North shore of Lake Huron. The Serpent River Indian Band in Ontario lived near the uranium mines of the heavily contaminated Elliot Lake region. The Serpent River system, including a dozen lakes, had by that time been identified as the largest contributor of radium contamination to the Great Lakes. Rosalie met with the Serpent River people on numerous occasions, documented their high rates of lung cancer and other illnesses in a report to the federal government, and inspired them to demand their rights. By displaying a conspicuous sign on a major highway—"Pollution is Her Majesty's gift to the First Nations"—they subsequently encouraged the government to clean up an abandoned sulfuric acid plant.

Rosalie also strongly supported the "Caribou Inuit" in their opposition to the proposed Kiggavik uranium mine in the Baker Lake region of the Northwest Territories. A local Citizens' Committee sprang up to resist the proposal of a German company to build an open-pit uranium mine upwind and upwater from Baker Lake. The Committee hired

Rosalie and two other experts to help them come up with precise wording for the questions they wanted answered during the environmental assessment process. Following public meetings, discussions, and workshops, the Citizens' Committee denounced the company's environmental impact statement, and the Kiggavik project was delayed indefinitely.

Canada, however, continues to have one of the world's largest inventories of low-level radioactive waste, scattered across sites remote from public scrutiny and awareness, and for the most part abandoned and unregulated.

Radiation Victims 2: Children

Rosalie's public speeches and writings consistently warned that children, more than any other group, are especially vulnerable to radiation and other forms of toxic pollution. During the 1980s, she carried out a number of investigations of environmental influences on the health of children. In Toronto, she first achieved a high profile with her investigation of radioactivity in suburban Scarborough.

In 1980, it was learned that residue from radium operations during the 1940s had radioactively contaminated the soil on McClure Crescent. Some of the current residents were experiencing health problems that they attributed to radioactivity in their homes and gardens. Despite official reassurances, residents began a class-action suit against the Ontario government for failing to warn them of the problem.

A lawyer representing some of the residents asked the IICPH for help. Film clips of the time show Rosalie checking out suburban homes, Geiger counter in hand. She also arranged testing for levels of lead-210, a radon decay product excreted in the urine of exposed children, and had laboratory work done at the University of Waterloo. A trend was found towards lowered white blood count with increased exposure to the gas and its decay products. Rosalie took this opportunity to point out that Canada was still clinging to outdated rules regarding permissible dose levels, despite recent changes in those levels elsewhere. By prevailing international standards, radioactivity on McClure Crescent exceeded permissible levels.

IICPH helped pressure the authorities into removing the contaminated soil and buying out many of the homeowners. Eventually, the government capitulated, compensating all those who wished to move. Rosalie considered this only a partial victory, however, since the government proceeded to rent out the homes at low rates. Tenants were required to sign a waiver absolving the government of all responsibility for any possible future health risks.

She studied a similar exposure of children to radioactive pollution at the site of a closed radium factory in Canonsburg, Pennsylvania, a city reporting a high number of childhood cancers, and one rated as among the most radioactively polluted sites in the United States. The factory's radioactive tailings pond had been capped and turned into a local base-ball diamond. Preliminary urinalyses of the children, performed at the University of Waterloo, showed a positive correlation between distance of residence from the dump site and the presence of uranium in urine.

She also examined the Brock West Municipal Waste Landfill, which was reported to be seriously leaking near Duffin's Creek, where area children played. Exposure to the creek was found to correlate with the risk of asthma and eczema. The government did not accept the study results, but acted to close the landfill.

Such cases gave Rosalie opportunities to transmit her message about the vulnerability of children to environmen-tal toxins and the need for change in public health services. "Public health departments are set up to deal with infectious disease and food poisoning. But what we are dealing with are toxic waste dumps, the local nuclear power plant, the pesti-cides, herbicides, and defoliants created for the Vietnam War. We are exposing the whole population to these mutagens and not even keeping track of what's happening." In order to assess the effects of a toxic environment, as when a poten-tially hazardous industry moves in, "Citizens need the protec-tion of baseline health studies—so you can prove change. You can't just say, 'All my neighbours are sick,' you have to say, 'These people were not sick before the nuclear industry moved in and they are sick now.'"

Testifying for Safer Radiation Standards

By the late 1980s, Rosalie's attacks on radiation standards and on the necessity of environmental monitoring were beginning to fall on more responsive ears in Canada. She pointed out that the International Committee on Radiation Protection (ICRP) was now the object of widespread criticism. It had accepted the findings of a study on the Japanese bomb survivors that showed humid weather conditions when the bombs were dropped had lessened the impact of radiation. ICRP conceded that the cancer risk was double that previously believed, but decided not to change the permissible dose levels. Their obduracy produced a split in the international consensus on standards of radiation safety when the British National Radiation Protection Board moved unilaterally to lower the permissible levels in the United Kingdom, stating that current levels posed a risk that "verges on the unacceptable."

Rosalie submitted a brief on behalf of the IICPH at an Ontario Nuclear Safety Review in 1988, highlighting these regulatory anomalies. She drew attention to recently published petitions signed by several hundred scientists, including biologists, who demanded that dose limitations be decreased by a divisor of 5, 10, or more. Even the magisterial science journal *Nature* opined that "ICRP is slower than it should be to respond to changing circumstances, and given to behaving as if its recommendations should be regarded as Mosaic tablets, to be accepted by all concerned with only the most laconic of explanations." Finally, in 1991, ICRP did lower the acceptable dose level. Most countries accepted them in practice, although some lagged in adopting them. Canada did not do so until seven years later.

However, the chairman's report on the 1988 hearing demonstrated that Rosalie's views were being heard, especially those concerning possible toxic effects to children. The chairman concurred with IICPH that more sensitive human health monitoring ought to be carried out "in the vicinity of nuclear installations with special emphasis on the health of newborns and young children. If there is any chance that the health of children is adversely affected by the nearby presence of a nuclear reactor, that fact should be established or authoritatively refuted."

Nuclear Weapons and "Atoms for Peace,"
Canadian Style

Despite the fact Canada had developed a "peaceful" nuclear program, Rosalie continued to argue that decoupling peaceful and military aspects of nuclear production is impossible in the real world. While living in the United States, she had long contended that nuclear energy was being promoted in part as a fig leaf for the weapons industry. "Nuclear weapons production requires public acceptance of its support industries, such as mining, milling, transportation, refining, enrichment, fabrication, deployment, decommissioning, and waste disposal. This total industry acceptance is, of course, automatic if the public accepts these industries as necessary for solving the energy crisis. Universities would hardly have a major in engineering weapons of mass destruction. Universities *will* train physicists and engineers to work for the 'peaceful atom.'"

Despite its announced policies to the contrary, she argued, Canada had been unable to avoid becoming entangled in nuclear weaponry, and her public statements frequently noted inconsistencies in government policy. She was also not averse to pointing out a tendency among the Canadian public towards passivity in the face of the powerful nuclear industry, and towards hypocrisy regarding its "peaceful" aims. "There is no incredible nuclear machine, it's just a bunch of people. We give it power when we declare ourselves helpless .... You can't give a mixed message. We don't want militarism, but we do want jobs under the defence-sharing agreement. You can't say both things: 'I'm for peace, but there's a lot of money in Star Wars so I'm going to do some research and make some quick bucks.' You are really choosing war when you do that."

There was no way, she insisted, that Canada could export uranium and nuclear reactors and guarantee that they would be used for peaceful purposes "The India experience," she noted, "does not give confidence that the reactor technology will not be used to develop weapons in Pakistan, Korea, and Argentina, which have contracted for CANDU reactors." She travelled to Nanaimo, British Columbia, to speak up for the protesters in Nanoose Bay, who opposed the US submarine arsenal near British Columbia waters. Repeatedly, she endorsed the Litton protesters who demonstrated against Canadian production of the guidance system for the cruise missile. "Are we willing to take responsibility for our societal actions or are we just for bandaging up the casualties? The Germans claimed ignorance of their concentration camps ... Americans claim ignorance of what their military occupation of Micronesia has meant. Canada claims ignorance about the uses of its component manufacturing and guidance systems. It is time to open our minds, seek the truth, and assume responsibility for the actions of our nation and our world."

Testifying in Britain:
Sizewell and the Greenham Common Women

During the early 1980s, through her repeated testimony at prominent inquiries, Rosalie became as well known in

Britain as she was in Canada. British journalists were attracted to the unusual combination of qualities she embodied. One reporter wrote, "She speaks in a down-to-earth, undramatic tone, without the least trace of bitterness or hysteria .... She handles the intensely emotional responses that her message causes, especially in women, with great compassion. She combines a paradoxical detachment from 'things of the world'—the power and remoteness of a scientist—with a real warmth and sense of humour that prevent her exuding any saintly piety."

Rosalie testified at Sizewell, the longest running British public inquiry in history. In the early 1980s, the local press had discovered high leukemia rates near Sizewell 1, a nuclear facility on the Suffolk coast. When Prime Minister Margaret Thatcher decided to construct Sizewell 2 as the first reactor in a program of nuclear expansion, public clamour erupted. Despite mountains of testimony over the years from local, anti-nuclear, and environmental groups, and notwithstanding the Chernobyl nuclear disaster in 1986 just as the final report was being drawn up, Sizewell II was approved. Only when Thatcher privatized the nuclear industry a few years later did expansion come to a halt. Nuclear power, unable to survive the cold scrutiny of the private sector, was judged too dangerous and costly to be an economic proposition.

The Greenham Common Women affair had a more successful outcome. In 1981, a group of English activists pioneered a novel protest tactic: they organized a women's peace camp at the United States Air Force base at Greenham Common to protest the locating of cruise missiles there. "As women we have been actively encouraged to stay at home and look up to men as our protectors," read an open letter urging other women to join, "but we reject this role. We cannot stand by while others are organizing to destroy life on our earth." Their appeal drew 30,000 Englishwomen to a protest at Greenham in December 1982. In a dazzling political gesture, the women encircled the base, holding hands and forming a human chain to prevent nuclear missiles from entering the base.

The peace camp was a media sensation, the first such anti-nuclear "happening" of its kind in Britain. The women camped out in the open air, winter after winter, danced around a missile silo, blockaded entrances and roadways, picnicked on the runway in teddy-bear suits. On New Year's Day, 1983, the women who had danced on the silo were arrested and charged with breach of the peace. Among the expert witnesses providing influential testimony on behalf of the women were Rosalie and Alice Stewart. Nevertheless, the women all went to jail. Rosalie recalls leaving the courtroom after a long and discouraging day, and later blurting out on national television: "I now know why the American colonists were disenchanted with British law and the Magna Carta." Eventually, however, this milestone protest succeeded in closing down the base and making it more difficult for the UK government to take over open spaces. It also provided a model for later peace camps, such as the one in Nanaimo, British Columbia, protesting the presence of American submarines in coastal waters.

Public and Professional Recognition

Rosalie received her first formal academic recognition in Canada in April 1985, when she was granted an honorary doctorate from Mount St. Vincent University in Halifax, Nova Scotia. A string of honorary degrees and awards followed from Canada, the United States, and India, recognizing her work for environmental and occupational health, and for peace.

In 1987, in her new hometown of Toronto, she was named Environmentalist of the Year, Woman of Distinction, and one of the Top 50 people in the city. As a newspaper account of the Top 50 award explained, "The names that kept coming up were those who motivate and activate, who move and stop things, who transcend their own sphere." The World Federalists of Canada gave her their World Peace Award in 1988, and she was also asked to become an adviser to the Great Lakes Health Effects Program of Health Canada, and to sit on the Ontario Environmental Assessment Board. In less than a decade, she had become an honoured and respected citizen of Canada.

These honours did not mean that disparagement of her work had halted. *Chatelaine*, a leading Canadian magazine for women, published a sympathetic article about Rosalie in 1987, mentioning recent critiques. A representative of the Canadian Nuclear Association slighted her academic credentials. "She hasn't published enough in scientific journals to have critical feedback from her peers." Certain health officials described her as "an alarmist who frightens everybody," and "a mathematician but no health expert."

Yet the nuclear industry was concerned about Rosalie's success in reaching the public. A secret AECL memo leaked to the press by environmental groups in 1988 showed that the nuclear industry took its critics much more seriously than their publicly dismissive statements suggested. The memo provided data on the financial status, membership, affiliations, strengths, and weaknesses of 20 environmental groups critical of the nuclear industry. It also went on to analyze how the opponents' strengths posed a threat, and whether their weaknesses might be exploited by AECL. The most striking analysis concerned Rosalie. AECL officials had always implied that her methods and conclusions were not to be trusted. The document, however, stated, "Dr. Rosalie Bertell is a world-renowned researcher in the field of leukemia and other cancer risks caused by nuclear power plants." It noted the publicity and credibility conferred upon her by the Right Livelihood Award (described on page 129), and the threat posed by the IICPH because Rosalie's work "receives media prominence, reinforcing negatives associated with the nuclear industry." The memo provoked a strong response from the Energy Minister, Marcel Masse, who warned he would not stand for attempts by the AECL to spy on or interfere with environmental groups opposing nuclear power.

Rosalie now had a strong support network in her adopted country and elsewhere. The succession of honorary degrees signalled academic recognition. She had also achieved public visibility and headlines: "A Nun for Our Times," "Nun Knocks Nukes," "A Cassandra For the Nuclear Age," "Bertell Rights Nuclear Wrongs." She appeared in National Film Board documentaries—*Speaking Our Peace* and *Nuclear Addiction*—produced by Academy Award–winning Montreal filmmaker Terre Nash.

People heard her speak at environmental hearings, peace groups, church and community organizations, and were exposed to her views on war and peace, the environment, and nuclear madness through the media. "Her impact," said colleague Ursula Franklin, "is far greater than one thinks. The very fact that people from utility companies now have to be prepared in case someone questions them about their procedures has reduced a significant amount of gross negligence."

Publishing: The Agony and the Ecstasy

Despite the wave of recognition and support, along with ever-increasing demands for her services as speaker and expert witness, Rosalie encountered repeated frustrations in one cherished aspect of her career identity: as writer and published researcher. It had long been important to her to have her credentials as a researcher and scientist validated by publication in peer-reviewed journals. She also cared about finding a wider audience for her findings, her opinions, and her message. The search for publication was often a humbling quest, with respect to scientific and popular publication alike.

A study Rosalie worked on in the late 1970s found "strong evidence" of a connection between radioactive gas releases from nuclear power generation in Wisconsin and infant mortality. When she sought the opinion of a Pennsylvania physician before submitting her results for publication, the reply was discouraging in the extreme: "I do not think the current paper will receive serious attention. To do a study that is going to be of interest to the wide scientific community, specific diseases and disease mechanisms must be identified. This cannot be done by reviewing death certificates."

In the early 1980s, Rosalie and two other Sisters produced a very different type of work, presumably conceived with a liberal Catholic readership in mind. *Shouting From the Rooftops: Women Religious and the Nuclear Age*, submitted to the Paulist Press, received a caustic evaluation from a managing editor who perhaps did not get around very much. "There are not many readers who really care that Sister So and So opposes nuclear arms and energy. Some lay people may find themselves resenting the ease with which Sisters can pop off to Europe, attend seminars and workshops, and otherwise devote themselves full time to some pressing social concern. None of the three stories provided were real 'conversion' stories .... Lacking in any conflict or indecision, they are not very interesting to read. Their responses are laudable but from a literary point of view boring. Our hearts are not moved."

Another cherished project was *The Handbook for Ionizing Radiation*, a detailed guide to estimating the health effects of ionizing radiation on different parts of the body. A reviewer for the University of Toronto Press sent back a careful and basically favourable report. Noting that the information was easy to find, well written, and presented in a logical, consistent, and coherent manner, the reviewer went on to say this:

> Dr. Bertell is an activist .... To those who disagree with her, and there are many in the established scientific community who do, her credibility is questionable. For this reason any document she authors has to be reviewed very carefully for either real or perceived biases in the report. The elimination of such biases is important, so that the natural antagonists to this author are not given, needlessly,

ammunition against a document that otherwise could be quite useful. There is no overt sermonizing or editorializing. However, there are innuendos and sentences that colour the overall tone. The tone of the document is to a degree alarmist and the author's biases do come through .... I still feel that the document should be published.

Rosalie agreed to make the manuscript conform to suggestions made by the reviewer but stated that she would not be free to do so for several months. In the end, it was published through the IICPH, with a second edition appearing two years later. In 1987, she sold the *Handbook* to a Japanese publisher. That same year she floated it on the American market—without success.

In 1980, Crossing Press had encouraged Rosalie to put some of her speeches together in the form of a book, tentatively entitled *The Dangers of Low-Level Radiation*. Two years later, the apologetic publisher wrote asking her to relieve him from the contract. "I can't see this manuscript adding up to a book. It is in pieces that range from personal to technical .... I feel to do the book would be a risk financially that I cannot take." Rosalie phoned in April accepting his decision, and deciding "to select and pull the book together" herself. She said, "It's on the back burner for now."

No Immediate Danger

Rosalie had been "selecting" and "pulling together" information about the hazards of radiation since 1976, when she took a year's retreat to contemplate her future life direction. Composed in the intervals of making a living and adapting to life in a new country, *No Immediate Danger: Prognosis for a Radioactive Earth* incorporated a decade of thought, research, and activism on the topic of radiation. It was finally published by Women's Press in London, England, in April 1985. Rosalie dedicated this book to her mother, "my best support." She recalls, "My mother read every word of *No Immediate Danger* (even the end notes) when she was 87 years old." It is an important achievement, which assembles a massive amount of scientific, political, and historic information. In its range, detail, and prophetic warning, it has been compared to Rachel Carson's *Silent Spring*.

Rosalie had engaged in negotiations with Women's Press for more than two years prior to publication. The book's title gestures ironically at the mantra that seemed to follow every nuclear accident or radiation spill: *there is no immediate danger.* Her publishers launched the book on April 25, 1985, and Rosalie embarked on a crowded schedule of readings, speeches, and media interviews throughout the United Kingdom. Journalists embellished the clash between the small, unpretentious nun and the formidable nuclear industry. "It is hard to believe that this woman is capable of making nuclear industry officials practically burst a blood vessel," ran one newspaper account. "She is slightly built, plainly dressed, with a slightly nasal voice and a friendly, unassuming manner." The book sold out on publication in Britain. In August, she was on the road again, promoting her book during a month-long set of engagements in Australia and New Zealand, where journalists accorded more print space to the "nuclear nun" herself than to the book, which nevertheless was positively received.

Some British readers were intimidated by the technical content in the book's opening chapters, but most were respectful of the book's scope and significance, "a dauntingly thick book but surprisingly readable." The *Guardian* called it "a sober technical account of the hidden horrors, past, present and future of the nuclear age," and included a lengthy account of Rosalie's career and struggles. In Britain, it was voted one of the best 20 peace books since 1945, and chosen by two Book of the Month clubs. The book was also released through Women's Press in Toronto, but failed to duplicate its British success in Canada. Rosalie contends that books are not adequately promoted in Canada, but recalls her own quixotic reaction when she did receive a grant to travel across Canada promoting the book: "I spent most of the money on travelling to the Northwest Territories, which is usually skipped by authors."

One year and a day after the book's release, the Chernobyl Number Four reactor in the Ukraine exploded. The resulting inferno spewed out a radioactive cloud for 10 days, releasing 100 times more radioactivity than the atomic bombs at Hiroshima and Nagasaki combined. This massive nuclear accident, the worst in history, gave heightened credibility to the book's warnings. Demand for *No Immediate Danger* skyrocketed as people sought to understand radioactive fallout. By the time Rosalie travelled to Britain in 1987, she had become a celebrity. In London, the *New Socialist* described her as the "world's foremost crusader against nuclear power." The Bath division of the British Medical Association invited her to speak at the president's annual meeting. This meeting, usually open only to members, was on this occasion open to the public. As the president noted, "We are expecting a big turnout for this important meeting .... There has been an enormous increase in public interest in the dangers of nuclear power since the tragic accident at Chernobyl last year .... We are most fortunate that Dr. Bertell has agreed to come and talk to us."

In the *Guardian*, eminent journalist Polly Toynbee wrote a lengthy article on Rosalie. She noted that Rosalie was a Grey Nun, "a fact only to be detected from a small crucifix of the order attached to her lapel. Otherwise, only a certain austerity in her manner and a quality of unshakeable certitude in her statements might indicate her vocation." Observing the difficulty of sifting conflicting data and interpretations about radiation dangers, Toynbee concluded: "Wherever you stand, Dr. Bertell's huge book on the subject—*No Immediate*

Danger—makes a terrifying read …. As long as the nuclear power industry propagandises so relentlessly, it is just as well that there are those like Dr. Bertell to challenge their complacency, and demand a more honest appraisal of the radiation risks to us all."

Even in the United States, where one publisher had turned her down because "your book is a bombshell and we don't want to be the ones to drop it," an edition was rushed to press, one that included a Chernobyl update. For the most part, it made few ripples in the United States. In 1988, Editions de La Pleine Lune in Montreal published it, with a preface by the well-known Québécoise novelist Marie-Claire Blais. The book was also translated into Swedish, German, Finnish, Japanese, and Russian. As Rosalie commented, "It has sold everywhere except in the US, where few people even know it exists."

The Right Livelihood Award: "Rogue Scientists" Recognized

The most important signal of international recognition in that decade occurred in 1986, when Rosalie received the prestigious Right Livelihood Award, along with Alice Stewart, the noted British epidemiologist. The "Alternative Nobel," better known in Europe than in North America, is conferred each year in Stockholm, one day before the Nobel Prize. First granted in 1980, the $25,000 award was established by a Swedish baron to honour those who have contributed to the betterment of society.

Congratulations poured in. A letter from Prime Minister Brian Mulroney, dated October 20, 1985, indicated the extent to which her adopted country had taken her to its heart and identified with her success. "Congratulations. This honour reminds each of us that, as tenants of this world, we are charged with its preservation and enrichment through applied research and active concern. Your dedication to the pursuit of excellence in the Environmental Health Field has brought pride and distinction to yourself, your colleagues, and your country. Through your invaluable work, you have contributed in a very substantial way to the betterment of our society and our environment."

Tributes from environmental, peace, feminist, and religious groups revealed the associations she had formed during her six years in Canada. The National Action Committee on the Status of Women (NAC), the venerable women's peace organization; Voice of Women, the International Joint Commission on the Great Lakes; Canadian Council on International Co-operation; Rev. Lois Wilson, past moderator of the United Church of Canada; and Dr. John Polanyi, professor and Nobel Prize winner in Chemistry at the University of Toronto, were among the many who sent telegrams and letters of tribute. The Grey Nuns' Sister House in Pennsylvania also felicitated their most famous living member, noting that she had "retained through all the public acclaim you have received, a spirit of Gospel simplicity and purpose," and the Superior General of the Grey Nuns made plans to attend the ceremony in Stockholm.

On December 8, 1986, Rosalie received the award in the Swedish parliament, along with a citation recognizing her for her "vision and work forming an essential contribution to making life more whole, healing our planet and uplifting humanity." The Canadian embassy put a car at her disposal, and held a special dinner in her honour, publicly demonstrating its support for a distinguished citizen. Dr. Alice Stewart, her co-winner, ruefully noted the contrast between the warm support Rosalie received from Canadian officials, and the chilly silence maintained by British representatives, who did not send a driver to pick her up at the airport, attend the ceremony, or even reply to an invitation.

In her speech of thanks, Rosalie expressed the hope that the award "to Dr. Alice Stewart and myself will mark a close to the era of global nuclear expansion and deception with respect to the hazards of ionizing radiation. I hope and pray that it will be the beginning of building the infrastructure of the forming global village." Certainly the award signified that major changes were afoot with respect to public knowledge about radiation and popular acceptance of the nuclear industry.

The Eroding Nuclear Image

During the 1980s, the dark side of the nuclear dream and its promoters became increasingly apparent. In Canada, the Atomic Energy Control Board (AECB) tried to increase permissible levels of radiation for workers and the public in 1983. When all the major unions united to oppose the changes, the proposal was withdrawn. However, the damage to public trust was never repaired.

At the same time, it became evident that the CANDU reactors were deteriorating more quickly than the experts had predicted, and that a lot of hazardous and expensive maintenance and repair work was necessary to keep deteriorating plants functioning. In 1983, a pressure tube suddenly burst in the 12-year-old Pickering 1 reactor near Toronto, despite previous assurances that such an event was impossible. Until this time, the CANDU had rated as one of the world's best reactor designs, engineered to last for decades. Both Pickering reactors were shut down while costly repairs were undertaken. Tube failures also caused the Bruce reactor to shut down, and the reactor at Douglas Point, on the shores of Lake Huron in southern Bruce County, to close permanently in 1983 after only 17 years of service.

Safety hazards in CANDU operations also came to light. Through the Freedom of Information Act, it was learned that for eight years the AECB had allowed the Bruce reactors to operate at a much higher power level than was considered safe by the Board's own regulations. Most damaging of all, studies showed increased leukemia near Pickering, and increases in infant mortality and birth defects, possibly linked to tritium emissions.

Yet another shock was the revelation that spent fuel from Chalk River was being used in military reactors to produce plutonium and tritium for US nuclear warheads, in flagrant disregard of the principle that the Canadian nuclear program was for peaceful purposes only.

Taken together, events like these undermined public confidence in the safety and the commercial viability of Canadian reactors, and in the commitment of the nuclear elite to public health and to the "peaceful atom." Yet the damage to the nuclear image in Canada was mild compared to what was unfolding in the United States.

In 1985, a new Secretary of Energy ordered safety inspections at 16 nuclear sites across the nation. Journalists and congressional committees took up the investigation, eventually discovering that there had been blatant disregard of the environment and workers' health at every nuclear facility. Contractors had jettisoned nuclear waste, dumping it into the closest body of water or burying it in the ground. For years, radioactive contamination had been seeping into the drinking water, soil, and air of neighbouring communities. In 1988, a hard-hitting series of articles in *The New York Times* drew the world's attention to the national disgrace. A congressional investigation that year led by Ohio senator John Glenn concluded, "We are poisoning our people in the name of national security."

Equally horrifying were the gradual revelations that an elaborate series of radiation experiments had been conducted on Americans, not only in laboratories but also at major American universities and medical centres. This unprecedented pattern of experiments began as part of the Manhattan Project, and continued for over three decades, driven by the wish to learn more about what radioactive substances would do to the human body. Contrary to official claims, not all experimental subjects were terminally ill. Young adults, including pregnant women and residents of prisons and homes for the mentally retarded, were among those involved. Congressman Edward Markey entitled the 1985 report of his subcommittee's hearing, "American Nuclear Guinea Pigs: Three Decades of Radiation Experiments on US Citizens." In her official admission of high-level wrongdoing in 1992, Energy Secretary Hazel O'Leary disclosed her own reaction: "The only thing I could think of was Nazi Germany."

It was a powerful indictment of an industry and an era: disregard of public and worker safety; poisoning of the environment; blocking of independent research; a culture of manipulation, secrecy, and lies, all justified in the interests of "national security." It was what Rosalie—long discounted by some as emotional, unscientific, extreme, radical—had been saying all along. Nuclear critics gained a more respectful hearing after this series of revelations. Moreover, particularly in the United States, they were joined by newly militant citizen and professional groups, determined to ensure that data gathering, radiation health research, and oversight would never again be left to the undisputed control of the nuclear industry.

The Wages of Success

Despite the awards, travels, and growing celebrity, Rosalie eked out a modest existence. Although she increased her fees, she spent most of the money earned from public appearances on the activities and publications of the IICPH, and on the monthly payments that all working Grey Nuns send to the Mother House in Pennsylvania to help support aged and infirm sisters. A letter to the editor of a book for which she was providing a chapter indicates how stringently she had to budget. On the topic of photographic illustrations for which she would have to pay, she writes that the chapter would have to go without photos. "I have not been able even to pay myself a salary at the Institute during the past two years."

An autobiographical article she wrote for a Japanese magazine in the late 1980s reveals how Rosalie saw the trajectory of her career since leaving Roswell in 1978. "The work has grown without funding or structure other than its own inner urgency for human survival. It is not a competitive or nationalistic survival, but rather a global interdependence which draws nations together in the crisis to give birth to a new way of relating internationally." Her own extensive international travels and commitments, particularly in the last decade of the century, aimed to advance that global vision of public and environmental health.

CHAPTER 6

THE GLOBALIZATION OF ROSALIE

After the publication of *No Immediate Danger* in 1985 and the Chernobyl catastrophe in 1986, demand for Rosalie's services soared. Her preferred activity was hands-on work with small groups of people, often in the developing world. In documenting health effects related to environmental hazards, as researcher, activist, witness, and friend, she created a deeply gratifying pattern of living.

Among Rosalie's many destinations during the 1980s, none made a more profound impression than the Marshall Islands in the Pacific. These are chains of coral reefs in Micronesia, halfway between Hawaii and Japan. After the Second World War, Micronesia became a United Nations Trust Territory administered by the United States, which undertook to "protect the inhabitants against the loss of their lands and resources." Between 1946 and 1958, the US tested 67 nuclear bombs on two of the islands, Bikini and Eniwetak.

The Bravo event in 1954 at Bikini was the largest ever detonation of a hydrogen bomb. It harmed not only the inhabitants, relocated to Rongelap and other nearby islands, but also many of the American servicemen who took part. Repeated massive testing caused lasting radiological contamination of all the test islands, and Bikini remains uninhabitable. High rates of thyroid cancer, birth defects, and Downs' Syndrome have been observed.

In organizing her trip to the Marshall Islands, Rosalie wanted first to assess local health needs by administering a health survey, modelled on the one she had developed to work with the Native people in Canada. As a follow-up, she proposed a program of assistance with medical personnel willing to donate two years' service to the Pacific region. A local official with whom she was corresponding remarked: "The Pacific Islands have had numerous researchers and professional experts fly in and out giving their advice or comments and then moving off never to be heard from again .... Also, airplanes are outstandingly unreliable." Rosalie was resolute, however. "While this may seem ambitious, I believe it will have to be done. Money will have to come from somewhere!"

In June and July of 1983, Rosalie arrived in Micronesia, accompanied by Sara Cate, a specialist in public health and epidemiology, and Colette Tardif, a nurse from Winnipeg. The women spent several days assessing radiogenic effects among the local populace and finding out what local health professionals knew about radiation effects. In January 1986, Rosalie spent a further two and a half weeks there, speaking with government and hospital officials, reviewing medical records, and assessing radiological damage among the Rongelap people. The hoped-for intervention with a team of doctors and nurses never took place, but Rosalie became a tireless advocate for the Marshallese people.

She was haunted by the memory of the Rongelap women who bore grotesquely deformed babies after the nuclear testing. The women had hytidiform moles—the people of the Marshall Islands called them "jellyfish babies." Says Rosalie: "It's like a living mass that's got some hair and some bones but no face and no limbs. It only lives as long as it's connected on the umbilical cord. So the woman would carry it for seven or eight months ... and she'd have this mole, just a blob of living material. One woman told me that she held her baby for three hours until it died and then she buried it so her husband wouldn't see it. So what you have here are women blaming themselves for having deformed babies."

Continuing witness by Rosalie and others kept the Micronesia issue alive in the US Congress, and the Marshallese citizens themselves organized and sued for damages. In 1989, Rosalie presented testimony before the House of Representatives in Washington about the health status of the Rongelap people. Government resistance to compensating victims weakened when previously classified documents revealed that AEC officials had intentionally returned the Marshallese to islands that they knew were still toxic, in order to study their bodies' reactions to life in a contaminated setting.

More than 1,000 radiation victims have received damages, and demands for compensation continue.

The Right to Health

Meeting the women of Rongelap strengthened Rosalie's conviction that radiation, and all forms of environmental pollution, systematically violated the rights of the vulnerable. In 1988, she and a group of concerned scientists set up the International Commission of Health Professionals (ICHP)—not to be confused with the IICPH—in Geneva. Its first yearbook published her address "Health As a Human Right." In it, she argued that human health, no less than civil liberties, was a human right. A fundamental right to uncontaminated food, air, and water should be as vigorously protected as civil rights such as free speech and free elections. Those least likely to enjoy this basic human right to health, she went on, were usually "a member of a minority group, indigenous people, the technologically illiterate, or generally politically weak." She was clear about the probable outcome if people continued to ignore the right to health. "Ultimately, if we do not address these fundamental health issues, the warriors among us, addicted with developing new forms of megadeath, will destroy us with slow poison, catastrophic environmental collapse, or all-out war."

Malaysia was one of the first countries in which Rosalie repeatedly testified to protect the health rights of a local population. Eight villagers in Bukit Merah brought a seven-year suit against the Asian Rare Earth (ARE) Company owned principally by the Japanese Mitsubishi Chemical Industries. ARE extracted rare materials from monazite to produce high-tech equipment for export. The resulting wastes contained a concentration of radioactive thorium and radium six times greater than the level internationally recognized as hazardous. As Rosalie described it, "[ARE] placed this dangerous material in plastic bags and discarded it in open trenches behind the plant. Dogs broke the bags open and dispersed the contaminants over a wide area, including land on which children played."

Local residents suffered cancers, leukemia, and birth defects. Rosalie was one of two scientists chosen to examine contamination of land and water, to assess the villagers' health, and to testify on their behalf. Members of the International Atomic Energy Agency, the ICRP, and Mitsubishi supported ARE throughout the lengthy court proceedings. The trial received international attention, particularly after it came to light that Mitsubishi had faced the same problems with a previous plant in Japan, where it had been ejected for pollution causing illness in the local population. The court eventually ruled against the company, ordering them to clean up and move out of Malaysia.

This ruling was the first of its kind in which a multinational giant was ordered to close because of negative health effects on local residents and environmental damage. When ARE attempted to stall execution of the court ruling, 10,000 residents demonstrated against their re-opening. "I have never seen such awareness and participation anywhere over an environmental issue," Rosalie commented later.

In her studies of health among the Bukit Merah population, as in her work with the Native peoples of Canada, Rosalie was developing a new methodology for looking directly at the health of communities affected by pollution. She called it "Health 2000" in honour of the WHO slogan "Health for All by the Year 2000." In 1991, the Ontario Premier's Council on Health presented her with a $200,000 Health Innovator Award, in recognition of this pioneering public health assessment tool. She put Health 2000 to use in a major survey of environmental pollution in the Philippines.

What Do Military Bases Owe Their Hosts?

For almost 100 years, the United States military occupied Philippine soil, and a US government department identified their Philippine bases as among the most contaminated in the world. In 1991, they closed the bases, without either cleaning up or disclosing their condition to the Philippine authorities. Each of 21 sites had at least one pollutant that exceeded drinking water standards, including mercury, lead, and solvents. Thirteen soil test sites confirmed unsafe levels of contaminants including PCBs, pesticides, and petroleum hydrocarbons.

Following American evacuation of one of the most polluted sites, Clark Air Base Command (CABCOM), the Philippine government set up a temporary shelter there for citizens who had been dispossessed by a volcano. Inhabitants were not advised of environmental hazards, and reports of vomiting, diarrhea, respiratory problems, and miscarriages began to arise.

In 1996, the People's Task Force For Bases Cleanup (PTFBC) decided to monitor the mounting health complaints. Rosalie Bertell and the IICPH were asked to perform a comprehensive survey, the first to examine the health of Clark residents. Over a period of two years, Rosalie studied environmental pollution in the area, and the health status of 751 women. Her report confirmed the presence of toxic contamination at Clark and revealed high levels of health problems in communities closest to the base. Contaminated water and soil were linked to kidney, urinary tract, respiratory, and nervous system problems. The survey recommended evacuation of residents until cleanup, soil decontamination, and clean drinking water could be assured.

These findings, as well as the ongoing efforts of Filipino activists, gained widespread attention. In December that year,

The New York Times brought the issue to the American public, noting that the United States had left dozens of highly polluted sites that "may now be the cause of disease among people living nearby. Washington has paid the Philippines nothing for cleanup and has released only perfunctory information about the hazards."

Individuals and organizations in the United States and around the world rallied to support cleanup of toxic bases in the Philippines and elsewhere. In 2000, a group of Filipinos filed a class-action suit against Washington. For Rosalie, the most gratifying results of the anti-base campaign were the boosts it gave to local activism and to international awareness of environmental crimes.

What Do Multinationals Owe Employees?

In the early hours of December 3, 1984, in the densely populated Bhopal region of central India, one of the worst industrial disasters in history took place. A pesticide plant owned by Union Carbide leaked a highly toxic cloud of methylisocyanate (MIC) into the air. More than 2,000 people were killed immediately, and over 600,000 injured. Union Carbide failed to clean up the site adequately, and the rusty, desolate complex continues today to leak poisonous substances into water and soil.

The gas, a volatile and dangerous compound, was stored improperly. Union Carbide had neither implemented previous suggestions for resolving accidents, nor supplied emergency response information to local authorities. The accident cost the company nothing, since their insurance covered the claims eventually awarded. Payments to individuals were insufficient to pay for the chronic ailments they developed, and many received nothing. The Union Carbide CEO, Warren Anderson, was indicted and released on bail, and he flew back to the United States, later refusing to return to India for trial. Union Carbide shut down its Bhopal plant and left. Later, the company agreed to place 20 primary health care centres in the community.

In October 1993, the Permanent People's Tribunal (PPT), an independent forum that convenes periodically to examine specific violations of the rights of peoples, met in Bhopal. It established a medical commission under Rosalie's leadership with a mandate to investigate the survivors' medical problems, their treatment, and compensation. With the assistance of activist groups in Bhopal, London, and New York, Rosalie sent out about 60 invitations to universities and research establishments. They chose 13 physicians from 11 different countries and with different expertise, each of whom served without pay, other than travel costs and expenses.

Thus, 10 years after the accident, an epidemiological survey was finally set up to examine illnesses in the local population. The results showed links between closeness to the factory and respiratory illness, neurotoxicological damage, corneal damage, and post-traumatic stress. Rosalie was scathing about the lack of emergency preparedness and medical information following the disaster. "Not filing data on toxics and potential hazards with local officials and emergency personnel is unethical and outrageous behaviour. MIC breaks down into cyanide poisoning in the body. The hospital had an antidote for cyanide. It was three days before anyone got information on that fact."

With respect to treatment, the commission found that instead of receiving chronic care and economic assistance, survivors often got "irrational, unnecessary and costly drugs." The lesson that commission members drew from Bhopal was that a global economy requires global rules: minimum universal standards with respect to a safe working environment, binding on all companies. Such standards must be based on the bedrock principle that companies should not harm people or the environment, and ultimately should be enforceable by the United Nations.

In 2001, Union Carbide ceased to exist, absorbed by Dow Chemical.

In 2003, a group of Bhopal victims, their previous claim in the US court system dismissed, filed an appeal.

Who Judges the Severity of Nuclear Accidents?
Chernobyl and After

The world's largest nuclear accident, the explosion and fire at the Chernobyl Number Four reactor in 1986, produced the greatest single release of radioactivity in history. It spewed radioactive iodine-131, cesium-137, strontium-90, and pluto-nium-239 all over the world, contaminating parts of Europe and the former Soviet Union more than all previous weapons tests combined.

More than 135,000 people were evacuated. The soil, in one of the world's top agricultural areas, could no longer be farmed. Because of inadequate monitoring, many areas of Europe were not recognized as contaminated until weeks or months later, and warnings about radioactive produce were introduced late or not at all. Only years later did the public learn that Belarus, because of prevailing winds, had been the most seriously contaminated area of all.

The regime of secrecy immediately instituted by the Soviet and successor governments sought, with American support, to deny and minimize the damage inflicted. A death toll of 32 was announced by Soviet authorities, who blamed the mount-ing toll of sickness on "stress." Each of the countries most affected, the successor states of Russia, the Ukraine, and Belarus, had its own political reasons for concealing the extent of the tragedy. Regulatory agencies such as the IAEA and the

ICRP, zealous to maintain the viability of nuclear power, backed up the political authorities. A leading American radiation researcher, however, spoke out. Dr. John Gofman estimated in 1986 that there would be almost half a million fatal cancers resulting from Chernobyl, and an equal number of non-fatal cases, both inside and outside the ex-Soviet Union. A decade later, having studied the health data available from the affected areas, he stood by those predictions.

Rosalie visited Kiev in 1986, soon after the explosion. She later kept in touch with Soviet scientists and tried to fathom discrepancies between official estimates of damage and those produced by independent researchers, some of them eventually silenced by imprisonment. Working with the Rotary Club of Toronto, she travelled to Kiev again in the spring of 1991. With her were a physician from the University of Toronto and a representative of the Children of Chernobyl Canadian Fund, who explored medical collaboration with appropriate health agencies, and later sent medical equipment.

In 1996, at another meeting of the Permanent Peoples' Tribunal (PPT), Rosalie was chosen to head up the International Medical Commission on Chernobyl. This meeting, co-sponsored by Physicians for Social Responsibility and International Physicians for the Prevention of Nuclear War, convoked 40 international witnesses to examine the consequences of the Chernobyl catastrophe.

Rosalie's own testimony described the scene of her latest

visit to Kiev: "On the tenth anniversary of the Chernobyl disaster, I was standing at a public meeting in Kiev, listening to the story of one of the firemen employed to clean up after the explosion. About 600,000 men were conscripted as Chernobyl 'liquidators.' They lifted pieces of radioactive metal with their bare hands ... they had to fight more than 300 fires ... they buried trucks, fire engines, and cars; they felled a forest and removed topsoil." Among the liquidators, 237 were immediately hospitalized and 32 died. None of the others was registered by name nor checked for subsequent health. They all went back to their homes, and many died.

The verdict and recommendations of the PPT were sent in 1997 to the health ministers attending a meeting of the WHO in Geneva. It noted that the PPT was "very concerned by the biased reports of the follow-up of the Chernobyl catastrophe and by the continuation of the world-wide promotion of the commercial atomic industry." Concluding that every step of the nuclear cycle was "associated with the production of dangerous, carcinogenic, teratogenic (embryo damaging), and mutagenic (mutation causing) substances," the Tribunal demanded a ban on nuclear power, and the withdrawal of a mandate given to the IAEA to promote nuclear energy. Moreover, they said, the ICRP should no longer be considered authoritative on health matters. Instead, WHO itself should gain complete control on reports regarding radiation effects, and establish regulations to protect human health.

The Chernobyl story continues. By the turn of the century, childhood rates of thyroid cancer in the most affected areas were 200 times those in Western Europe, and congenital abnormalities were turning up in the children of those irradiated by Chernobyl. With every year, the scale of the damage has expanded, particularly as more advanced techniques of biological measurement have become available.

Each of these distant undertakings—in Malaysia, India, the Philippines, and the Ukraine—highlighted the inadequate management of problems that are transnational in scope. Each, in Rosalie's view, demonstrated the urgency of developing international regulations and structures.

Pushing the Limits of Personal Sustainability

Although friends and colleagues were amazed at Rosalie's energy, the extensive long-distance travelling took its toll. Indeed, she challenged her physical health in ways that would have taxed a younger, stronger woman. From the mid-1980s, in her letters and faxes back home, there are references to illness. In July 1985, she wrote, "I leave for Japan and the 40th anniversary of Hiroshima and Nagasaki. Then to Australia for the launching of my book, *No Immediate Danger*, then to the Philippines for the licensing hearing for the Bataan reactor and then to Papeete in French Polynesia to help the people resist the French nuclear weapon testing there. I will be back in Toronto about the 26th of September. I hope you are well. I have been quite sick (a collapsed lung) and feeling 'low energy.'"

In a June 1987 letter to a journal editor, she thanks him for pruning her article, "which (as usual) I wrote under time pressure and illness. I have had lobar pneumonia again after climbing around a radiation dump in Malaysia with a Geiger counter. My belief in respiratory damage coupled with lowered resistance to disease as radiation effects has been reinforced." A fax to her office in Toronto about a planned visit to India and South Africa notes: "It looks as if I can get back from South Africa on the 16th of February and leave for Texas on the 19th. I have to return on the 23rd for a meeting in Windsor. This is all if my health holds up."

The effects of packed speaking schedules, transportation vagaries, unaccustomed foods, and environmental hazards were increasingly reflected in illness. One year, she suffered three bouts of pneumonia. On another occasion, when her travel schedule called for stops in Hiroshima, Nagasaki, Hong Kong, Bombay, Muscat, Nairobi, and Kinshasa, she was forced to cancel most of her engagements. From a convent in Tokyo she faxed her office that she was under doctor's orders to take at least a week to recover from a severe case of shingles. In 1992, just before shooting commenced for a *Women in Science* video, Rosalie observed that she was having foot surgery and might still be on crutches during the filming. Her comment was characteristic. "We can work around this!"

She knew she was pushing her limits, however. This awareness surfaced in a talk she gave in Norway in 1990. Comparing the environmental concept of sustainable development to the personal experience, she said, "If you have gotten beyond youth and good health and suddenly have to confront chronic illness, you begin to realize what it is to sustain what you are doing. The kind of work you do, the amount of sleep, the amount of food, the number of new undertakings, are very much limited by your personal energy and your personal ability to sustain it."

Yet she continued to take on more speaking engagements and new projects, driven by her sense of mission, and by new threats she perceived to planetary survival, including depleted uranium (DU).

Depleted Uranium: From Waste to Weapon

During the 1990s, and even before, Rosalie's was one of the earliest and strongest voices raised against depleted uranium (DU). Used for the first time by the United States and Britain in the first Gulf War, DU is made from the radioactive wastes left over from making H-bombs and nuclear reactor fuel. Composed of 99 percent uranium-238, which has a half-life of 4.5 billion years, DU weapons have been used in both Gulf Wars, Afghanistan, and the Balkan War.

Radioactive and chemically toxic, DU is heavier than lead or steel and therefore unmatched for use in missiles, munitions, and tank armour. In the words of Pentagon officials, DU blasts through tanks "like a hot knife through butter." On impact, DU munitions burn and disintegrate to uranium oxide dust and smoke, which can travel kilometres on the wind, before settling on the earth. "So-called 'precision bombing' is a cruel hoax when DU is used," says Rosalie, "because its dispersion is uncontrollable." Rosalie points out that the UN Human Rights Tribunal has included DU weapons among weapons of mass destruction, and they are therefore incompatible with human rights law.

DU can be inhaled or ingested in soluble, insoluble, and ceramic (glass-like) forms. The soluble forms pass through the body in hours, but ceramic DU, once inhaled, can stay in the body, irradiating tissue, for years. During the first Gulf War, bombing left many tons of uranium-238, mostly in Southern Iraq, where it will contaminate the soil, water, and food chain forever. American troops were not monitored for radiation exposure or warned of the dangers of DU.

Predictably, the health impact has been severe. In Iraq, there are increased cancers in all age groups, especially among children. The same pattern is emerging in Bosnia and Kosovo. The Gulf War Syndrome experienced by over

150,000 American veterans was likely caused by a number of toxic threats, including massive vaccinations and burning oil wells. But the syndrome also includes many symptoms common to victims of radiation contamination: immune-deficiency infections, leukemia and other cancers, and reproductive problems among female partners of exposed veterans, who experienced miscarriages, infant mortality, and birth defects. DU has been detected as much as eight years later in the semen and urine of veterans.

Rosalie revealed the duplicity of American and British governments in downplaying the impact of DU, although the dangers were well known. Not until 1998 did the Pentagon acknowledge that thousands of US soldiers might have been exposed. Accordingly, in the second Gulf War, the troops were warned to bandage all cuts, and to keep their rubber suits zipped tight.

Rosalie also publicized Canadian DU connections. Canadian veterans, too, suffered from Gulf War Syndrome, and Canada contributed to DU production by sending uranium to the United States to remove the fissionable U-235 component required to make fuel for nuclear bombs and reactors, a process called "enrichment." Says Rosalie: "If we do not ask for the depleted uranium to be returned within 30 days, it becomes US property. The radioactive waste can then be used for weapons."

Brave New Weapons: HAARP, ELF, and More

As the 20th century drew to a close, Rosalie's attention shifted from nuclear weaponry to radically new American war strategies that involve the planet itself as a weapon. Her last book, *Planet Earth: The Latest Weapon of War* (2001), presents a wealth of information on how war and military testing are disrupting natural patterns both on the earth and in the protective layers of the atmosphere. "It is hard to scare or shock me with evidence of technological madness in our world," wrote Elizabeth May, executive director of the Sierra Club of Canada, in her review of *Planet Earth*. "I am immersed in the evidence. But Rosalie Bertell's new book made me feel naïve."

One startling project is HAARP (High-frequency Active Auroral Research Program), an installation in Alaska that, in Rosalie's words, "is related to 50 years of intensive and increasingly destructive programs to understand and control the upper atmosphere." This grid of powerful antennae and transmission towers is capable of bombarding the atmosphere with high-frequency rays, creating "controlled local modifications of the ionosphere" (outer layer of the atmosphere). A US Air Force study points to the use of such modifications as a means of altering weather patterns and disrupting enemy communications and radar.

The main military purpose of HAARP is to heat sections of the ionosphere until they bulge to form a curved "lens."

This will reflect HAARP's massive energy beams back to earth, destroying selected targets—presumably without leaving a trace of what caused the devastation. Now operational, HAARP has the ability to potentially trigger floods, droughts, hurricanes, and earthquakes. Scientists have warned that no one can fully predict the impact of such operations, which could affect both brain and behaviour.

Planet Earth describes how HAARP and installations in Russia, on which the United States has collaborated, can also create pulsed, extremely low-frequency (ELF) waves. These have been directed deep into the earth itself, potentially disrupting delicately poised tectonic plates of the earth's crust, such as the San Andreas Fault. There is, moreover, a growing chain of extremely powerful, potentially interactive military installations, using varied types of electromagnetic fields or wavelengths, each with a different ability to affect the earth or its atmosphere. Their effects on the earth's core or the atmosphere are impossible to predict, but many have speculated that testing of this new technology is related to recent earthquakes and freak weather patterns.

Former US Secretary of Defence William Cohen has discussed the possible threats of military experiments that affect the earth and its atmosphere, claiming that "others" are engaging in an eco-type terrorism whereby they can alter the climate, and set off earthquakes and volcanoes remotely, through the use of electromagnetic waves. As Rosalie observes, "The military has a habit of accusing others of having capabilities they already hold!"

Peace, Environment, and the Energies of Women

By the early 1990s, Rosalie had become a global figure, and her advocacy for the environment was recognized in 1993 when the United Nations Environmental Programme (UNEP) placed her on the Global 500 Roll of Honour. Her speeches and writings focused increasingly on three interrelated issues: a basic human right to health, the dangers of militarism, and the role of women in promoting peaceful pathways to international security. She had become more outspoken, among other things, on the exclusion of women from decision-making about peace and war.

From the beginning of her activist career, Rosalie had observed the preponderance of women in her audiences. As she commented at her first nuclear reactor hearing: "Maybe it's concern for life." Throughout her career, women formed the majority of her support system. They invited her to speak, helped organize her trips, provided hospitality, published her first book, called on her for TV, radio, and newspaper interviews, offered their friendship.

From the mid-1970s onwards, in groups such as the Clamshell Alliance and the Greenham Common peace camp, women had assumed leadership roles in anti-nuclear and ecological groups. According to Rosalie's friend, Petra Kelly, former leader of the West German Greens, "[W]omen all over the world are rising up, infusing the anti-nuclear, peace, and alternative movements with a vitality and creativity never seen before."

As early as 1985, at the Women's International Peace Conference, Rosalie had condemned existing peace negotiations and recommended that negotiating teams be composed of men and women who would work for more equitable distribution of the world's resources.

During the 1990s, focusing on the dangers of militarism, Rosalie sought increasingly to engage women in the growing threats she perceived to peace and planetary health. She attended several major conferences organized by and for women, usually as the keynote speaker. These gatherings, in Canada, the United States, Europe, and China, testified to the increasing confidence and involvement of women in political life.

At the 1995 Beijing Conference on Women, Rosalie examined many of the major themes that had preoccupied her during the past decade: the impact of modern technological warfare on the human habitat and life-support system, the growing threats of the military mind-set, and the socioeconomic costs of war. Rejecting the argument that war and violence are "natural," a changeless component of human psyche and history, she stated, "Violence is not natural. Many external forces are required to keep the killing activity in place: special uniforms, better food ... punishment of deserters ... elaborate social pressures. The myth of war being a part of human nature needs to be exposed as a lie .... It is behaviour which needs to be renounced, just as civilized people renounced slavery and cannibalism."

Throughout this period, she used the metaphor of addiction to describe societal assent to military ways of thinking. "It has all the classic signs of an addiction. It's secretive and exaggerated, it sacrifices health and social goods, it takes the best and finest young brains in the country and drains them off into producing weapons of mass destruction. This addiction to militarism is widely destructive and we are not confronting it."

She believed that mainstream environmental thinking—reduce, reuse, recycle—too often focuses on relatively minor issues. "When we talk about an environmental problem, we say that it's everyone's refrigerator, their underarm deodorant, or it's because they don't recycle paper. We don't say anything about the major things the military is doing to damage the life-support system."

Rosalie saw hope in the numerous groups working to promote fundamental change: international organizations of indigenous peoples; labour organizations; religious, medical, and environmental groups. Above all, she put her trust in the energies of women who made up the backbone of the environmental and peace movements, and promoted norms of co-operation and non-violence.

Scaling Down

Rosalie decided to step down from the IICPH in 1994, while continuing to pursue her interest in community health on a limited and personal basis. A ceremony in November of that year marked both the 10th anniversary of the organization and Rosalie's retirement. In a final letter to Institute friends and supporters, Rosalie announced that in celebrating a decade's work in IICPH, she and the board were particularly gratified by model programs they had pioneered to foster human and environmental health, including the Health Impact Assessment Surveys, and the Health 2000 methodology used both in Canada and in distant settings like Malaysia.

In a final letter to the Institute's supporters, Rosalie wrote:

> Our 10-year celebration also has a sad note as I have requested the Board to accept my resignation because of ill health. I feel good about what has been and I hope that the models which are now visible and viable will attract others to carry on the work. Thank you for your long time loyalty. Remember always the power which flowed from working together on good things. Your continued support of IICPH will be essential to its continued vitality.

Since 1995, the IICPH has continued in existence as an "institute without walls," and Rosalie has maintained her ties with it. As recently as 2003, at age 74, she participated at an IICPH conference in Toronto.

As her health continued to decline, Rosalie decided to make one more move. She returned to Buffalo in 2001, where family and friends from her earliest years welcomed her back after two decades of adventures in Canada and the wider world. Travelling and speaking engagements became fewer in number, but did not stop entirely. She dedicated herself to completing *Planet Earth: The Latest Weapon of War*, which was published that same year.

Also in 2001, the International Peace Bureau, the world's oldest peace organization, awarded her the Sean McBride Peace Prize. The testimonial accompanying a silver medal honoured "her work with indigenous and developing country peoples to preserve their human right to health and life in the face of industrial, technological, and military pollution." She was selected by the International Biographical Centre in Cambridge, UK, for inclusion in its publication *2,000 Outstanding Women of the Twentieth Century*.

CHAPTER 7

DREAMS BIGGER THAN A LIFETIME

Among Rosalie's treasured documents is a letter she received from Sir Kelvin Spencer, former chief scientist for Britain's Ministry of Power. He wrote to her in 1984, following her testimony at the British Sizewell nuclear inquiry:

> I write to you with the cheekiness and growing immaturity which sometimes accompany old age. I am an ordinary citizen, a retired and time-expired scientist, who notes with sadness the lack of intellectual honesty in many who owe allegiance to the nuclear industry. Your paper to the Sizewell inquiry is what has been wanted for decades, but only now, thanks to you, has been brought into existence. All of us and our even more numerous descendants, have and will have cause to give you thanks, and learn from you how to devote one's life to a self-imposed and exacting task. You have, I know, already faced many attacks, misrepresentations, subtle insults, and many direct insults too. So my excuse in writing is in the hope

it will give you a momentary bit of pleasure to know that there are many who admire you but few of them who will get down to a typewriter and tell you so. You are indeed a worthy successor of such personalities as Florence Nightingale and Rachel Carson.

Indeed, the similarities among the three women's lives are striking. All survived sickly childhoods, eschewed marriage, and devoted themselves to careers related to public health. In doing so, they directly challenged the male elites of their times, and were subjected to harsh denigration as a result. In Rosalie's case, she attacked the integrity of the scientific, governmental, and corporate establishments, their moral leadership and direction of society, exposing their careless-ness with human health and the natural world. It was a message that the establishment had to neutralize, for it could lead to withdrawal of public support for a powerful industry, to damage claims and lawsuits, to a loss of public confidence in society's decision-makers.

Thus, her assault on nuclear science, technology, and policy-making—all dominated by males—was met by a relentless barrage of criticism. She was not a "real" scientist, but a number-cruncher who had lost her academic creden-tials. She wrote for the public, thus compromising her scien-tific credibility. She employed stories, anecdotes, and personal references in her speeches and writings, the sort of "evidence" that has no place in science. She was a nun and a woman. By preferentially addressing her as "Sister Bertell," her detractors downplayed her professional expertise, conveying the notion that she was embedded in a spiritual realm remote from the world of science. Sacrificing reason to sentimentality, she propounded exaggerated arguments born of oversensitivity to the inevitable sufferings of humanity. Her pronouncements on radiation lacked value.

And yet, she seems to have been right more often than wrong, and both public acceptance of nuclear energy and scientific opinion have been moving in her direction over the past decades.

The Decline and Fall of Nuclear Energy?

Rosalie's activist successes came initially from focusing on two points: the damaging health effects of radiation from nuclear reactors, and the inadequacy of public protection afforded by the International Commission on Radiation Protection (ICRP). In the early 1970s, nuclear reactor construction was in full swing in North America, and the ICRP a magisterial source of regulatory wisdom. Today, nuclear power has lost public acceptability throughout most of the Western world, and the ICRP appears on the defensive.

Reactors continue to be built in the developing world,

particularly in India and China. In Western Europe and North America, however, construction is at a standstill. Despite the stated intent of the current US administration to promote nuclear reactor construction, no serious movement in that direction has yet occurred. In Canada, the troubled nuclear industry, centred in the province of Ontario, may be experiencing terminal throes. Early in 2004, the minister of energy for that province announced that his future policies would focus on energy conservation, and on renewable power sources such as wind and solar energy. Public health concerns about reactor safety, the insoluble problem of nuclear wastes, and the astronomical costs to the taxpayer of constructing, repairing, and decommissioning nuclear plants make the future of nuclear reactor construction uncertain. It would be premature, however, to proclaim the death of the nuclear industry in Canada. Atomic Energy of Canada Limited (AECL) continues to promote the construction of new reactors, and the view that nuclear energy is a solution to global warming.

As to the fundamental question of what levels of radiation are "acceptable," criticism of the ICRP approach is no longer confined to "rogue scientists." A new generation of researchers, including scientists working within the academic establishment, question ICRP standards and models of research. They contend that it is not scientifically permissible to extend the data on external radiation, based on the atomic bomb studies, to the kinds of internal doses received by such populations as nuclear workers and people living downwind of nuclear sites. The ICRP paradigm was based on physics and evolved before the discovery of DNA and the development of molecular biology. The emerging paradigm, based on biology and epidemiology, deploys advances in testing techniques that have, for example, enabled the measurements of mutation rates in DNA of children conceived following Chernobyl by parents who had helped clean up after the explosion.

ICRP is now modifying its tone and its message. Reports are underway on issues to which Rosalie drew attention for decades: monitoring for internal exposure of workers, cancer risk at low doses, radiation risks to embryo and fetus, the practice of taking the adult male as the basis for calculating radiation risk. ICRP also plans to issue yet another new set of dose recommendations in 2005. "We must become better at keeping the public as well as our peers informed," stated Dr. Jack Valentin, scientific secretary of the ICRP, in a recent policy statement posted on the Internet.

Thus, changes are visible, in policy decisions on nuclear energy, in scientific understanding of radiation risks, and in the tenor of ICRP pronouncements. However, irreversible contamination of the environment and the gene pool has already occurred. By allowing technology to outdistance knowledge, mistakes have been made for all time.

Part of a Great Chain of People

Rosalie's path led her from monastery to graduate studies and teaching, from cancer research to nuclear energy critic, and to global activism for peace and environmental protection. A career arc marked by change and discontinuity, not unusual among women, was further complicated in Rosalie's case by her uncertain health and her religious vocation.

She faced multiple crises that seemed to shut the door on growth and achievement. Yet each time, she shaped new openings for herself. When she suffered congestive heart failure in the monastery and renounced the contemplative life, she went on to undertake graduate studies with great distinction, and to become a beloved teacher. Another episode of illness, along with the wish to use her advanced training, caused her to leave teaching and embrace cancer research. Increasingly aware of the dangers of low-level ionizing radiation, she turned towards anti-nuclear activism, while continuing her scientific work. As she approached her fiftieth birthday, mounting criticism, loss of research funding, and threats to her physical safety left her without job, colleagues, or support. Her response was to create her own job, first in Buffalo, and then in Toronto, as an independent consultant, speaker, and researcher.

It was never easy. "People don't realize how dependent scientists are; they have no idea," she once said. "Who pays the scientist? Government, industry, the university—and they don't fund controversial projects. Scientists need grants, equipment, resources ... Most of the time you're living on the edge, with barely enough to keep yourself going." Yet Rosalie was adept at creating positive outcomes in the most unpromising circumstances. From her experience of "living on the edge," she plucked autonomy and independence. "I live on next to nothing—that makes it hard for people to put the usual pressures on me."

The constants throughout Rosalie's career were her searching intelligence, her capacity for unremitting hard work, and her passion to be "fruitful," to make a difference in the lives of others. She took her knowledge of radiation to her audiences and encouraged them to stand up and protect themselves. "I am amazed at citizen groups who know at a gut level when they're being affected and hurt. No matter how much propaganda is flying around, the public is some-how getting a message about the dangers, and the lack of trustworthiness within government and industry circles that are saying everything's fine."

People intimidated and talked down to by the "experts" recognized an ally in Rosalie. She told them they were right to fear nuclear contamination, and to embrace the duties of informing themselves and sharing information with others. Terry Wolfwood, a British Columbia activist and writer, recalls Rosalie's energizing presentation at the Beijing

Women's Forum in 1995. "The one thing she said that I will never forget was that we all have a responsibility to seek information and the truth, and we should always listen first to our sisters who are in the midst of an event. She said also we have the responsibility to transmit vital information: 'We can be our own media.'"

Rosalie brought many assets to her speaking engagements: her encyclopedic knowledge of radiation and the nuclear industry, her moral passion, her ability to engage different types of audiences, her gifts of humour and storytelling. Diverse observers—sophisticated journalists, worried parents, close friends—also recognized her outstanding personal qualities: sincerity, simplicity, and kindness. Wolfwood, who has known Rosalie for two decades, remarks that "in spite of her deserved global recognition, she's no diva. She answers her own mail and telephone, she always expresses personal concern, she is unfailingly modest about herself, and she is generous with her time and wisdom."

In late 2003, awaiting cardiac surgery, Rosalie was working on a chapter entitled "In What Do I Place My Trust?" for an as yet unpublished book in which activists discuss the beliefs that help them to remain hopeful in troubled times. In her words,

> The continuity of life, the call for making things better for the next and the next generations blots out all hesitation.

To act becomes natural, and to not be able to act, a torment. We do not need to enjoy the fruits of our longing, as we "see" them taking fruit in others who will come after us. We are part of a great chain of people who care about the Earth, about the life that gives it fruitfulness, and about a world where rights would be respected, children cherished, and peace prevail. We have to be part of something larger than ourselves, because our dreams are often bigger than our lifetimes.

LIST OF PHOTOGRAPHS

Page 6: Rosalie Bertell (age five) with her great aunt, Sister Rosalie Wolfe. Providence Retreat, Buffalo, New York. Photo credit: Rosalie Bertell's collection.

Page 26: Rosalie Bertell with her parents. House of Studies Catholic University, Washington, DC, 1962. Photo credit: Rosalie Bertell's collection.

Page 83: Rosalie Bertell created the Ministry of Concern for Public Health in 1978. Photo credit: Rosalie Bertell's collection.

Page 100: Rosalie Bertell came to live in Canada in 1980. Photo credit: Rosalie Bertell's collection.

Page 157: "My mother told me to curl my hair because it would 'soften' my hard message!" 1990. Photo credit: Rosalie Bertell's collection.

Page 160: Rosalie Bertell, Victoria, BC, 1999. Photo credit: Theresa J. Wolfwood.

Page 171: Rosalie Bertell and fellow honorary degree recipients during St. Francis Xavier University's Spring Convocation. Antigonish, Nova Scotia, May 2, 2004. Photo credit: St. Francis Xavier University.

Page 171: Rosalie Bertell receives an honorary degree from St. Francis Xavier University. Antigonish, Nova Scotia, May 2, 2004. Photo credit: St. Francis Xavier University.

SUGGESTIONS FOR FURTHER READING

Books

Bertell, Rosalie. *No Immediate Danger: Prognosis for a Radioactive Earth.* Weaving together scientific, political, and historical information, this ground-breaking account presents the dangers of ionizing radiation to an international audience. Toronto: Women's Press, 1985.

Bertell, Rosalie. *Planet Earth: The Latest Weapon of War: A Critical Study into the Military and the Environment.* Calling for a new approach to global security, Bertell argues that advanced military and space research and programs—from electromagnetic weapons to "Star Wars"—threaten to destabilize the ecosystem, generating environmental and economic havoc. Montreal: Black Rose Books, 2001.

Blowers, Andrew, et al. *The International Politics of Nuclear Waste.* Scholarly analysis of public policy formation in Europe and North America regarding radiation waste disposal, the "Achilles heel of the nuclear movement." New York: St. Martin's Press, 1991.

Caufield, Catherine. *Multiple Exposures: Chronicles of the Radiation Age.* Engagingly written, brilliantly researched account of the history of radiation, and the many mistakes and accidents along the path to better understanding its biological effects. Chicago: University of Chicago Press, 1989.

Giangrande, Carole. *Nuclear North: The People, The Regions, and the Arms Race.* A CBC journalist crossed Canada talking to workers and executives in factories and nuclear plants, native uranium miners, and ordinary citizens about nuclear reactors, missile testing, and Canadian involvement in the nuclear arms race. Toronto: Anansi, 1983.

Greene, Gayle. *The Woman Who Knew Too Much: Alice Stewart and the Secrets of Radiation.* A gracefully written biography recounting the life of a remarkable British physician whose pioneering research suggested a link between radiation and childhood cancer. Ann Arbor: University of Michigan Press, 1999.

Laird, Gordon. *Power: Journeys Across an Energy Nation.* An informative account of Canada's varied and abundant sources of power—including nuclear energy—and the problems and prospects of each. Narrated with a storyteller's eye for striking detail and revealing anecdote. Toronto: Penguin Canada, 2002.

Lifton, Jay, and Greg Mitchell. *Hiroshima in America: A Half Century of Denial.* Summarizes the controversies about why the atomic bomb was employed, and speculates on how the silence and deception surrounding its use have affected the American people. New York: Avon, 1998.

Websites

www.atomicarchive.com
A high quality, accessible site presenting the science and history of nuclear energy, along with photos, diagrams, and reading suggestions.

www.ccnr.org
Comprehensive website of the Canadian Coalition for Nuclear Responsibility, covering the history of nuclear energy in Canada, and topics such as uranium mining, reactor safety, radiation waste, nuclear weapons, and energy alternatives, from a Canadian perspective.

www.thebulletin.org
Founded by a group of Manhattan Project scientists, the Bulletin of the Atomic Scientists has warned the world of nuclear dangers since 1945, providing non-technical, scientifically sound information about nuclear issues and global security.

RABBITS
AND
REDCOATS

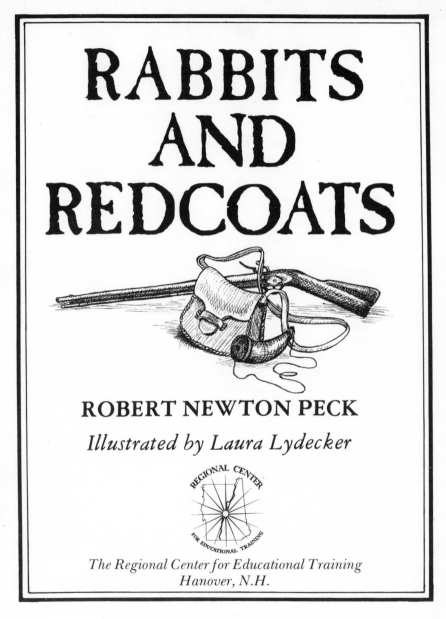

ROBERT NEWTON PECK

Illustrated by Laura Lydecker

The Regional Center for Educational Training
Hanover, N.H.

PHOTO CREDITS: Richard K. Dean. Reprinted courtesy of the
Fort Ticonderoga Museum.

Text Copyright © 1976 by Robert Newton Peck
Illustrations Copyright © 1976 by Laura Lydecker

Hard cover edition published
by Walker & Co., New York

Paperback edition published by the Regional Center for Educational Training as a title in the Bicentennial Historiettes Series of the New Hampshire-Vermont Bicentennial Educational Resources. All rights reserved. No part of this book may be reproduced in any form without permission in writing from the publisher, except for brief quotations contained in a review.

The publication of the paperback edition of RABBITS AND REDCOATS has been made possible, in part, by grants in aid from the New Hampshire American Revolution Bicentennial Commission, the Vermont Bicentennial Commission, and the New Hampshire Commission on the Arts.

LIBRARY OF CONGRESS CATALOGING IN PUBLICATION DATA

Peck, Robert Newton.
  Rabbits and redcoats.

  SUMMARY: In May 1775 two boys participate in the capture of Fort Ticonderoga by Ethan Allen and the Green Mountain Boys and befriend a young British soldier.
  1. Ticonderoga, N.Y.—History—Capture, 1775—Fiction. 2. United States—History—Revolution, 1775—1783—Fiction I. Lydecker, Laura. II. Title.
PZ7.P339Rab pb. [Fic] 75-43449
ISBN 0-915892-06-5   paperback

Printed in the United States of America

RABBITS AND REDCOATS

Books by Robert Newton Peck

*Special thanks to Jane Lape
and the Fort Ticonderoga Museum
for all their help.*

To every boy before a battle

FORT TICONDEROGA

How defiant a fortress can be.

This fort was a cocked fist, rock hard and ready to strike, armed with the toughest soldiers to ever level a musket, the British Redcoats.

Fort Ticonderoga in 1775 flew British colors, stood sturdy on a point of land, looking eastward to Verdmont as if to shout—"Come take me, if you have the bowels." Her holler slapped the face of Verdmont farmers, men and women and children who held their own land against attacks by weather, wilderness, and red savages from the north. But each Verdmont family was also a fort.

The bloody history of Ticonderoga began in 1609, when Samuel de Champlain committed a giant military blunder, one that cost France her northern kingdom. With two other Frenchmen and five dozen Indians (mostly Huron) he led a force south from Canada in twenty-four canoes. Landing near Ticonderoga, they were confronted with the Iroquois. But instead of befriending these redmen as the French usually did so readily, Champlain fired his arquebus and killed three chiefs. One shot, and New France was never to be.

Iroquois hatred for the French persisted, and the five nations (Iroquois) became allies of the British, aiding them to victory in the French and Indian War. Before that war, in 1755, a fort was built by the French at Ticonderoga, and she was called Fort Carillon.

In 1758, General Abercromby of England attacked General Montcalm's Carillon with a formidable force of 15,000 men, mostly Highlanders of the Black Watch.

In 1759, General Amherst defeated General Montcalm, and Carillon became known as Fort Ticonderoga, the most strategic stronghold in early America.

For nearly two decades, little happened at Fort Ti. Until, across the lake, a Verdmonter named Ethan Allen mobilized a small striking force of farmers, the Green Mountain Boys. Their plan, suicidal though it sounded, was to rowboat over and capture Fort Ti, in 1775, for the American cause.

Already our Yankee Doodles had been whipped by the British, three times, at Lexington and Concord and Bunker Hill. But assisted by Benedict Arnold and some Massachusetts troops, Ethan Allen waded his men ashore, and to their destiny.

Rabbits and Redcoats is about this early turning point in the American Revolution. More action at Fort Ti would follow; but those stories are many, and for other books to tell.

By the way, have you ever been to up-state New York and seen Fort Ticonderoga as it is today? It's worth a trip.

Fort Ticonderoga is fully restored, with much of the original stone used by the French engineers in 1755, when it was called Fort Carillon. As you walk her barricades, an emotion may invade your heart. Is it pride? I have been to Fort Ti a hundred times, and I will go again, as each trek mysteriously stiffens my spine. I stand taller when my hand touches the black barrels of cannon, and the cold rough stone of that great gray star.

Laugh if you will at my history high. Yet my spirit lifts, and silently my ear marches to its own private fantasy of fifes. Pangs of a patriot? Perhaps, yet I want you to share it with me. Please go there. Stand on a high wall and command Fort Ticonderoga, see her and touch her and harken to her silent bagpipes and to her distant and dusty drums.

Feel it? You are still . . . an American.

R.N.P.

Fort Ticonderoga looking south, up
Lake Champlain

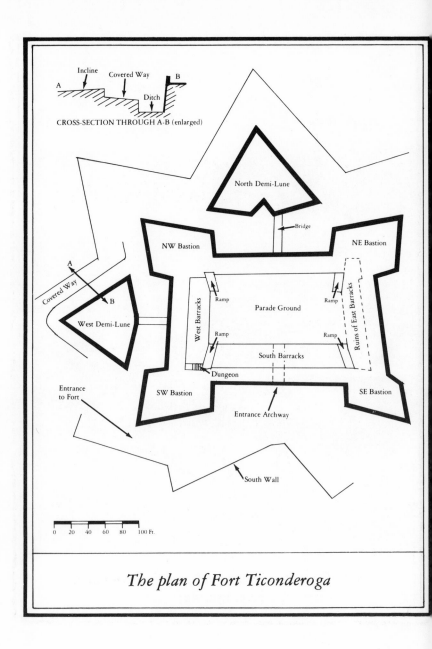

CROSS-SECTION THROUGH A-B (enlarged)

Incline Covered Way

A

B

Ditch

North Demi-Lune

Bridge

NW Bastion

NE Bastion

Covered Way

A

B

West Demi-Lune

West Barracks

Ramp

Ramp

Parade Ground

Ruins of East Barracks

Ramp

Ramp

South Barracks

Dungeon

Entrance
to Fort

SW Bastion

Entrance Archway

SE Bastion

South Wall

0   20   40   60   80   100 Ft.

The plan of Fort Ticonderoga

6

Fort Ticonderoga and the surrounding area

Ethan Allen

Benedict Arnold

CHAPTER

1

"Are you scared?"

"I don't guess I ever been more so," I said to Interest. There was water on the hickory stock of my musket. I wiped it with a wet hand. Sure was a dark night, especially under the lakeshore trees.

"You ain't fixing to turn tail? Or be sick?"

I shook my head, figuring that if Interest Wheelock had the bowels to join up with Ethan, then I had the grit to do likewise. Now that it was May, I was nigh to

sixteen and almost as old as my friend.
But not near as tall.

"No," I whispered to Interest. There
was no moon at that moment and the Verdmont swamp was sure lonely. A bug bit
my neck and I cuffed him dead. "We got
guns," I said, trying to deepen my voice,
"same as the rest." Just as I said it, I
heard a fox bark from away off, like that
old red was laughing at us.

There was no moon at that moment and the
Verdmont swamp was sure lonely.

"Yeah, but yours is for rabbit."

"Who said?"

"I can tell. And I wager Ethan Allen and all them bigwigs could spot the difference right off," said Interest.

"Not in this dark. You could be my own dear ma and I'd not know it."

"Hey, were your folks asleep when you snuck out?"

"Yup," I said. "Were yours?"

"Like they sat at sermon."

The way Interest said stuff always made me giggle. I was sure glad that he was along. For awhile he'd left me to spy on what the officers were doing, down by the boats.

"Who'd ya see besides Ethan?" I asked him.

"Saw a smaller fella. He spoke of Connecticut like it was home to him. Heard some voice call him Benedict."

"What in a thundering's a Benedict?" I asked, scratching a bug bite.

"Maybe a major or like that. Chapter?"

"Yeah."

"Them boys is really going to do it.

Dang! Sure wish we'd joined up proper, so's we be a Green Mountain Boy in . . . in . . ."

"In good standing," I said. "Well, I was for it. But you wanted to work the dog that night and run coon."

"We treed her."

"So dogged high we never saw sight of her again, and that dumb dog of yourn backtracked halfway to Middlebury."

"Don't call Blue a dumb dog," said Interest.

"I won't," I said. "Blue's ever bit as smart as you."

"Be right back," said Interest. "Stay put."

Holding his musket, he snaked his big frame through the trees. The moon came out, but once again I was alone, listening to the bugs, and smelling the damp of the bracken. Must of been bugs by the hundred dozen score, all piping a fresh tune. When I heard the soft whirr, my head whipped around real sudden, to see about the biggest old heron I ever seed light down easy, with just a whistle of

14

wings. Then he froze, lifting up a foot like he was fixed to wait Christmas.

Ba-riggy!

The cowfrog surfaced about two musket lengths away from the motionless heron. But I'd bet a bonnet he saw that frog, even though he dassn't twitch a feather. Just the cowfrog's head poked up from the black water, sending out little rings of ripples. Big mistake, cowfrog. That's what I was studying to myself. You come right under his sword. A big mistake.

And that's what we're probable to make, the two of us.

Interest Wheelock and Chapter Harrow ought to lie home asleep on their own cornhusk. Laid and lofted as my mother would put it. But no, here we are in some swamp, waiting to mix in with some Greenies, so's we can brag on how we nightrode with Ethan the time he took Ti. Well, maybe me an' old Interest can pull it off. Nobody'll be the wiser in the darksome. And if we git ourselves caught, the most Ethan can do to us is to pack us home to our mothers.

A moment earlier, only one leg of the heron was in sight. But now the coiled foot had dropped, so slowly that the frog and I took no note. The heron saw the frog for sure. Just like all them Redcoats over crosslake at Fort Ticonderoga will see us Verdmonters coming in our boats. Come to meet us? No, they'll just wait. And let us move in under their guns. Yes, the heron's foot was moving even though it was so cussed slow you'd swear it was still as ice. Down, slowly the free foot dropped down, until the long toes touched the water, and now the great heron was one step closer to the cowfrog.

A whole step, and yet I could near to take oath that the heron had not moved.

One more step would bring that old heron close enough to strike. The great neck would snap forward, too fast for the eye to follow, and the sword of his beak would stab his supper. Did the cowfrog see the bird? If so, why didn't she swim away to safety in the dark water of Lake Champlain? Inch by inch, the wet foot, on which the heron first stood, lifted up to cross its

16

mate, then, to snail its descent closer to the frog. Patience, my father once said, is what the heron could teach us all. And that a farmer has to grow patience along with his other crops.

I don't want to be a farmer.

I want to be a journalist, a writer like Samuel Adams in Boston. And I sure don't cotton to be a soldier if this is what soldiers do, set a swamp and swat bugs. One wee devil was biting my face, yet I dassn't budge for fear of spooking either the cowfrog or the heron, or both; wanting to see what would happen without my spoiling their business. Closer, closer, closer . . . the eye of the heron fixed on his meal. My cheek took a smart as the skeeter sucked my blood. It didn't hurt. All it took was a might of getting used to, and on the morrow I'd bear a pink lump where the bug had bited. Would I be alive tomorrow? And would Interest Wheelock also be? Will I have to musket a Britisher and cut down on him? I pray I shall not.

Interest and I had been crosslake to

trade at Fort Ti many times, and we has talked with some of the young British soldiers. Lads no older than we. One was called Peter Geer, and he could sing with a more than fair voice. He sang a song once about a lass who served tankards of rum in a Newcastle tavern that hung the sign of the Scarlet Goose. The girl knew many men and all who heard his song laughed in good nature. I had laughed whenever Interest had done likewise.

Now I felt little like mirth, and I did not want to discharge a musket at Geer. Yet I wish to play a part to free my country, as Samuel Adams had said. He wrote in a copy of the Boston *Gazette* that one man should not slave for another, not even for King George.

Father did not like Samuel Adams.

Once he remarked that in his opinion, Sam could stir up more smoke than heat. Nevertheless, some day I would journey to Boston Town and go to Purchase Street just to shake the hand of Samuel Adams, hoping that he might extend to me advice on how a farmer's son like myself might one day learn the craft of penmanship. I should cotton to sign Chapter Harrow to a poem or an article writ by my hand that he might read.

"Chap!"

The cowfrog jumped, just as the rapier of a heron's bill slashed downward, picking into the mud in the very spot where the frog had been. A clear miss! With a loud squawk of protest, big wings opened and off he flew, still hungry, into the fog of Lake Champlain.

"What's afoot?" I asked Interest.

"They sure do lip a good fight. Seems like a dispute's cropped up twixt Ethan and this Benedict fella, the one who brung them Massachusetts troops."

"How do you know that?"

"I heard tell."

"Are they loaded in the boats yet?"

"Soon."

"It'll be daylight 'fore we go," I said.

Interest Wheelock scratched his bare head, like he was thinking on something. "Yeah, little bud, and that ain't good. I don't guess I want to walk up under them black holes even in dawn light."

"Me neither. What black holes?"

"All the mouths of them English cannon. They got near to a hundred tons of brass over yonder, and I reckon a good share of them howitzers is aimed at us Verdmont folk."

Supper come up in my throat. For an instant, I had to reswallow Mama's parsnips and fatbelly pork. A sour taste.

"You scared?" asked Interest.

"Naw, not so much as to back off. My hands sure do wet up my musket stock a mite. How come you keep asking? You scared?"

"Me? Well, I don't guess I want to die with a lie on my lips, so I'll fess it out. My hands don't shake, so nobody'll really cogitate on how frighted I am until Mama goes to wash my britches." Interest give a grin.

"Come on," I said. "Let's work ourselves closer to the boats. Where are they?"

"Through the alders. Well hid. All we got to do is sort of stir in like we belong."

We crept forward toward the lakeshore, moving slowly with patience, as a heron might wade. I wondered if I was a heron or a frog.

CHAPTER 2

"That's some fog."

Except for the steady creak of the oars, Interest Wheelock's whisper into my ear was the only sound on the lake. Except for the rush of water that passed beneath the belly of our boat.

As we rowed, we faced the Verdmont shore instead of where we was headed which was crosslake to the York side. That's why, I told myself, when I git myself a boat it'll be an Injun canoe in which a man can look the way he goes. But old

Interest was right. Never had I seen a meaner morning fog on Lake Champlain.

"Thick as porridge," I whispered back.

A big boot kicked my butt. Not hard, but I knew quick off that the burly oarsman at my back had enough of our boyish prattle and wanted to hear no more. Interest give a grin my way as he pulled his oar, like to say how pleasured he was it was *my* arse that stopped the shoe. Dang his hide. There sure was moments that I hated Interest Wheelock. He was tall and I was short. And he owned his own mare and musket. But we'd growed up together, fast as willows, the Wheelocks and the Harrows being near neighbors; so I sort of took the idea that next to Interest I come out second best. Yet we were friends.

He also said he's kissed Molly Painter. And pinched her a few times.

When I'd go uploft at night, sometimes my eyes would close and then I'd see his face next to her face. And then I'd come along and call him out and fist him proper. After that, I'd kiss Molly Painter's sweet cheek, but I wouldn't tell anybody about it. I wouldn't want a soul to know. Just her. If only it weren't just a dumb old dream. You are so fair, my Molly Painter.

Suddenly, I felt a big beard at my ear, and a deep warning. "Boy, don't hurry your oar. Keep cadence with us rest."

When the prow of our boat hit shore, I heard the grind of sand under the keel. Jumping over the gunwale, I splashed through the fog toward the black of the shore trees, making a rousing racket. I figured every Redcoat at Fort Ti must of give ear to it. I dang near run up the back of a big man, stepping on his heel. As he turned, I scooted off toward the pucker-bush, but I knew it was Ethan. At least he failed to recognize me. Or so I thought, until I felt a big hand rest heavy on my shoulder.

"Chapter Harrow," his deep voice said.

"Yes, sir, Mister Allen."

"I am Colonel Allen. But first off, why the devil are you present in this company?"

"Well, we . . . I sort of . . ."

"Are others with you who are not

24

"Chapter Harrow, why the devil are you present in this company?"

sworn members of our force?" He looked around, his eye falling on Interest Wheelock. "Is that not Isaiah Wheelock's son?"

"Yes, Colonel." The pork and parsnips came halfway up once again.

"Dammit to Jehovah!" Ethan could whisper an oath sharper than a common man could holler. "How many of you . . . you dang *squatters*, we got?"

"Just us pair."

"Cuss it, I ought to leather the brace of you boys to a tree and leave you here. If'n I weren't friendly with your fathers, I holy would."

This was a bent truth. I knew dog well why Ethan wasn't going to do too much to me. It was on account of Hetty. She was my older sister, and still a spinster at eighteen. Some said that Hester Harrow was the prettiest lass in Shoreham. Ethan had smiled her way more than once and touched his hat as he bowed. He was wedded, but folks said that Ethan Allen would hardly let such a low hurdle as wedlock trip up his way. Mama wasn't too surprised as Ethan smiled at Hetty. What

26

took her back was when my sister smiled back.

In less than a week, Ethan stopped by our place. As he pretended to talk to my father, I took note of how much looking Ethan Allen performed over Papa's shoulder.

"You two lads," said Ethan, "stay behind our column and well to the rear. And you are responsible for each other, hear?"

"Yes, Colonel Allen." I saluted.

Raising his arm, he played as if to cuff me proper; but instead, he lowered his hand only to muss my hair. Yet not gently. Interest Wheelock watched the doings, figuring, I suppose, that he'd get the next tan. Ethan splashed off to the south, muttering "damn squatters."

Guess as old Ethan was in the property business, him and his brothers and their Onion River Land Company, he took a dim view of folks who'd squat in unpaid land. Families who bought from the Allens always paid up, or got burned up. Ethan put a torch to more than one debtor.

All of the Verdmont and Massachusetts troops moved off to the left, to the southward, headed toward where they reckon Fort Ticonderoga stood its ground. Interest and I followed. It sure was mucky footing. And the marsh gas was a sorry smell. Bugs all over. No moon. I wanted to reach out and touch somebody. This swamp sure could make a sad place to get left behind in. Looked to me as if our count was about seventy or eighty. Hard to tell in the fog. A man on my right was commanding the rear guard. Papa knew him. His name was Seth Warner.

As I looked to the eastward, the sky over Verdmont was graying to dawn. Best we hurry or lose the night.

I saw Fort Ticonderoga.

Above us on a rise of ground was the great gray star of stone. The French had built it, twenty years back, or so the story goes. Then the British nabbed it. General Amherst took it over from General Montcalm. I wondered if Ethan Allen would be a general. Who made him a colonel? We Verdmonters didn't have an army. Heck, we weren't even a colony yet. Not according to what the New Hampshire people claim, and the Yorkers. Each say we're theirs. But we ain't. Long as we got Ethan we'll be free. And the New Yorkers can whistle for their tribute. Ethan said that to my father and they both had laughed.

I wish Papa would talk more about politics.

Is he a Whig or a Tory? I asked him once. He answered, "Why? So you can brand a 'W' or a 'T' on my brow with a hot iron? Is it not enough that I am a Verdmont farmer?" He spoke no more of the matter; and all the rest of that one day, he and I worked splitting plank. And I knew better than to crowd him. I had once cornered a stoat. A grave error, as I was stoutly bitten.

"Chapter? Hey, Chap!"

"We're supposed to hush up," I told Interest.

"Lordy, look at that row of cannon."

"What do you think I look at? As if a man could advance toward a British fortress and see other."

We saw a long row of black holes, each one a mouth that could madden at any moment. I wondered as I ran forward in my sloshing shoes, carrying my rabbit gun, which black hole would be first to redden with death.

As we run forward toward the great gray wall that grew higher and higher, the only dry thing about me was my mouth. My rabbit musket must have weighed a ton. I prayed to the Lord we'd reach that wall.

All I saw was cannon.

"Chapter." Interest's breath was so labored he could hardly get out the words. "There's something I got to tell."

"Best you tell it fast," I said, my running feet dodging around the stone that had probable been scattered in this open for just such a purpose.

"I never done kiss Molly."

CHAPTER

3

One gate was a small door.

For some reason, it was unlocked and unguarded; and man by man, all four score of us ducked through it, and up a steep bank. Me and Interest were last through the gate. Muskets held high, we crossed an open area toward the black opening of a large tunnel beneath the south barrack.

Only one shot got fired. But I saw no man fall.

Yet at any moment I expected to feel a

half a pound of British lead tear through my breast. We were such a tattered troop. How could we ever be a match for British Redcoats? Interest ran a step to the front of me as we poured through the dark of the arch and into the courtyard. We heard shouts. But not from our boys. The cries of alarm were from English throats, sudden screams of ladies, followed by a bark of a dog or two. Then came the soft low of a milk cow to lift my spirit, as the sound said that back yonder was a Verdmont morning. Papa would milk Agnes and wonder where I had gone.

He would know. News of our capture of Fort Ti would fly fast.

Interest and I broke a run across the big courtyard of Fort Ticonderoga that was north of the archway we'd just ducked through. Neither of us knew which way to go, or whether to cut down on a British soldier. Didn't see but three of them Redcoats and all three had their hands in the air, and not a musket betwixt them. Their mouths was wide open like they didn't know what to say or shout. Nobody shot nobody. I couldn't understand it. All we heard back home in Verdmont was how many Redcoats we was going to send upstairs to the Benefactor, but I don't guess too many of us was cotton to do it personal.

Sure was a passel of hollering. Most of it come from up yonder in the west barrack. Some poor souls was making a fuss over our sudden arriving, for sure and for certain. The look on the face of Interest Wheelock said that he was just as blustered about matters as I was. Just then a British regular, without his red tunic, come out a door. There was a saber in one fist and a lit lantern in the other, which silvered the blade of his sword. I couldn't think of what to do, so I just put the muzzle of my wee trusty right up under his English chin to give his jaw a tap to remember.

"Surrender," I ordered him.

"In whose name?" he looked at me.

"Verdmont and the Lord God," I told the man.

"Don't shoot him, Chapter. Yer ma'll

have a cow if'n you do, and you doggone know it," said Interest. "You already shot over a dozen. Ain't that enough?"

That old pal of mine sure could fib when his mind was to it.

"Best you surrender, sir," I said again, "or die."

He dropped his sword.

My hands were at a tremble, and I can't ever recall my old rabbit gun being so hefty. All of a moment a warm and wet feeling trickled into my britches before I had the mind to turn it off. I felt like a dang fool.

"Sit down, mister," I heard Interest tell the soldier, "or else I'll turn this killer loose on ya." He jerked his thumb at me.

"What do you intend?" he asked.

"Sure wish I knew," Interest answered him. He held his musket sighted at the white of the man's blouse, while I looked around. At last I could breathe easy. Sure was glad I didn't trigger that Britisher and slew him. Mama would of raised Cain. And then Papa would take me apart and leave me in bits, not to mention double all my chores. Everywhere I looked, British soldiers held their hands high in the air. We prodded our captive so he'd join his fellows.

"I can't believe all this," said Interest.

"Nor can I."

"And yours ain't the only rabbit gun we brung over. Sure enough ain't."

"We caught the Redcoats with their britches off."

"The war's over," said Interest. Throwing back his head he give out with a good old Green Mountain whoop. The faces of some captured Britishers turned ashen. I can wager when an ear first hears a mountain scream it might give a body the goose bumps, as it was half Injun.

I looked for our friend, Peter Geer.

The sun came up, cracking over the edge of the Verdmont horizon to split apart the heaven and the earth. A day to divide England and America. We struck their colors. Down come the Union Jack. I was grateful that my father did not see my role in this action, as he had always raised up both Hester and me to honor the British flag.

Verdmont men entered one barrack after another, coming out with armloads of loot. One carried a bundle of bedding. Another toted muskets. We found their magazine. Among the kegs of black powder lay a box of flints, a handful of which I put into my pocket. To do so gave me an ill feeling; and so a moment later, I returned the flints to their box. I wanted to be a soldier, not a thief.

Interest found a barrel of winter apples, still firm and ripe, as they had been quartered well. "Here ya go," he said, tossing me a shiny Jilliflower. We sat on a stone battlement and bit into breakfast.

"Interest?"

"That's me."

"Do you think this'll crank up a war?"

"Maybe so. But if'n it does, I pity them Redcoats if this is the best they can scrap."

"Don't be an idiot, son," said a voice.

We both turned around to see an officer in uniform, standing behind us.

Holding a fresh map, he looked north, up Lake Champlain toward Crown Point and beyond to Canada. My face must have begged his identity.

"I am Colonel Benedict Arnold, so mark me. These soldiers are the dregs. The cracks are with Billy Howe in Boston, and with Gage. And up there."

He pointed north.

"Ain't nothin' up yonder but swamp," said Interest, looking my way with a snort and a smirk.

"Perhaps to you," said Colonel Arnold. "But for me, there is far more. Even my destiny."

"Like what?" I said.

"I look north, my lads, thinking of one man."

"Who is it, sir?"

"John Burgoyne."

"He a Verdmonter?" Interest spat out an apple pip.

Colonel Arnold smiled and let out a sigh. "Hardly. He is an English general. And if I am as much soldier as he, I must throw myself and a lot of lads like you into the spokes of his chariot. Perhaps it will be General Howe who will attack us from the north. Yet my bones say it will be John Burgoyne."

Folding his map, Colonel Arnold touched us each on the shoulder. Light as a roe, he jumped down off the fort wall and hurried off. He sure could wear that red uniform, muddy though it be. Actually it was part blue and creamy yellow, but the red trim on the collar and cuff was what caught your eye.

"You read that there gink?" Interest asked me.

"No, not real. But someday I think I will. Did you sop up all he talked about?"

"Not one word."

A man run by us carrying a commode of polished cherry wood that shined like Sunday silver. Somewhere a woman screamed. We heard bottles smashing and men laughing. A Massachusetts man offered us a drink from a jug. Interest took a good long pull, made a face, and tried to gag it down. Then I drank. Sure was awful and it sure weren't rum. I took an-

Then I drank. Sure was awful and it sure weren't rum.

other deep swig in hopes it would grow on me. It didn't.

"What is this stuff?" I asked the soldier.

"It's called gin. Want more?"

"You know," said Interest, "I don't even want what I got."

The soldier left us, swinging his jug of gin as it hung from his finger. His walk was unsteady. My eye followed his progress and saw him near to stumble into Colonel Allen who pushed him in the direction of the pump. The man fell and Ethan booted his backside. My father had advised me how little people favor a sot, and I could see Papa spoke true. The man was a mess. In the same glance I saw our friend Peter Geer who was standing straight, in uniform but unarmed. Funny thing, I thought, how a defeat can outshine victory.

"Hey," said Interest, "let's go see old Pete."

"Sure."

Hopping down from the wall we went over to where the captured British soldiers was lined up. Many were older than we, but some were near to our age. An older Verdmont man paced to and fro before the row of Regulars, shaking his musket at them and speaking abusive words. Pointing his musket in the face of Geer, the old man pretended like he was going to pull the trigger. Peter Geer closed his eyes.

"Don't," I said.

The man turned. "Who the heck be you?"

"My name is Chapter Harrow. I'm a Verdmont man like yourself . . . and a friend to Private Geer."

"Who?"

"This man."

"He's a Reddy!"

"My father and I come to trade at the Fort once or twice a season. We know some of these people. We know *him*."

"Be you a damn Tory?"

"No, I am a Whig." I felt dizzy. High-tone words were starting to swarm inside my head.

"A *what*?" His musket swung toward me.

41

"Don't," I said.
The man turned. "Who the heck be you?"

"A patriot. Like yourself, I believe in the freedom of all men, even the captured. I believe in Sam Adams and the Continental Congress and in Ethan Allen's Land Company. I believe in Verdmont as an independent colony. And I believe, sir, that unless you lower that there firing piece from my chest that . . . that . . ." My head was a jig.

"He's going to throw up," said Interest. "He does that a lot."

"What fer?"

"Gin."

"Huh?" It was easy to see that we had the old man confused. His musket sort of swung from Peter to me and Interest, like it couldn't sight on any one soul. He sure had hanker to gun somebody.

"He's a drunkard, sir," said Interest. "You can tell the way he talks, he's a souse. Pity the lad, sir. Him and me don't hold much courage like some of you older boys, so reckon the doings was a bit too much excitement. Chapter, you fixed to throw up?"

I held my stomach, trying not to bust

43

out laughing. But old Interest Wheelock weren't so lucky. His face cracked out a grin a rod wide.

"You tomfooling me?" The old man looked angry.

"No, sir," I said. Leaning forward, I whispered into the wax of his ear. "It's his mind, sir. Honest it be. See for yourself how he laughs like a loony when there is no wit. Like now. No joke's been told, yet see him giggle like a mad goat."

Interest made his goat noise, and it finished me.. I did bust out laughing. So did Peter. The gin come up my gullet, mixed in with pork and parsnips, the stench of swamp water on my shirt, and the taste of a Jilliflower apple. So I really did boot my breakfast, like a cannon, all over the sandy courtyard of Fort Ti. And fell forward. I thought Interest would die laughing.

"Bunch o' fools." The old soldier limped away.

CHAPTER

"We rescued Peter," I giggled, trying to get up.

Ethan come along with Ira his brother and he told us that no British soldier was to be harmed. Or sported with. That was when he saw me lying on the ground and raised me by hand on my neck scruff. It hurt some.

"What ails *you?*" Ethan sounded tuckered out.

"He's grieved," said Interest.

"From what?"

"Gin."

"Your old Puritan ma will render me, boy. And it ain't even my fault. God, kid, you smell like a summer sausage. Go wash him off and flush his gizzard. Chuck a bowl or two of hominy down his dang fool throat. It usual works for *me*. Get him to the pump."

"Yes, sir," said Interest.

"What's *your* name?" Ethan turned to our friend.

"Peter Geer, sir."

"Then lend a hand, Geer. Blood of Mary, how in hell old are *you?*"

"Sixteen, sir. Almost."

"What in tarnation are we doing in this dang war, turning kids into pit dogs? You oughta be home to England helping your ma and pa. Now git!" Ethan marched off, kicking the dust with his big wet boots.

Interest and Peter sort of drug me to the pump box, and pushed my head under a bit longer than breath could take. I come up in a sputter.

"Ugg!" I said.

"Sounds half Injun," said Interest.

46

"And half gin," said Peter, pulling me up.

"Ain't no curse on earth worse than a drunk redhide, as you can plum see, Pete. Let's dry him out and sober him up."

"I'm not . . . .". They ducked my head again.

Nothing seemed to cut real sharp. Reckon it was the gin. Interest took sick later in the day. Then we both stole a heck of a long nap on some grain sacks beneath the west barrack. Peter woke us up.

"What you been doing, Pete?"

"My wash." His hand on my shoulder smelled soapy. "If your officers ask if I am a soldier, I can answer an honest no. I am a scrubwoman."

"I'm hungry," I said. Interest said he was, too.

"Here," said Peter Geer, "I brought you a hunk o' mutton."

"Cold mutton," said Interest, "and hot gals. That's my style, boys."

The cold mutton was good. Then we went in search of something to wash it down. We found fresh milk, warm as a morning cow, and it tasted like home. With our six feet hanging over the high wall, the three of us sat on the cool stone and watched the sun back off from a May sky. It sure had been a long day. I yawned even more of it gone. We were eating apples.

Then we both stole a heck of a long nap on some grain sacks beneath the west barrack.

"Too bad," I said.

"What is?"

"It's too bad the three of us can't soldier in the same army."

"Aye," said Peter, "and for my opinion, pity we three cannot be *out* of the same army. Soldiering is not to my liking."

"What made you enlist, Peter?"

"I didn't."

"Then how come . . ."

"My family and I are farmers. But after dark one night in the town of Newcastle, I was bopped on the noggin, and when waking, found an advance of money planted in my pocket and myself unwilling in the King's service. Then off to America without as much as a bye-bye to my dear old mum. Was it the same with you?"

"Not us," said Interest.

"We just tag along," I said, "because we wanted to be in on the shoot. You know, to say we were there when Ethan took Ti."

"He can take it and welcome, for all of me," said Geer. "All I want is to sail

49

home. Pull up stakes and pack our duds.''

"You'll miss a war," I said to Peter.

"Why do you think thus?" There was no war in his eyes.

Fetching back my arm, I hurled my apple core as far downhill as it'd carry, yet far short of the lake. "Because there's a

Fetching back my arm, I hurled my apple core as far downhill as it'd carry.

spate of folks spoiling for a good fight. Over in Shoreham that's all you hear."

"War talk," said Interest Wheelock. "On account we all want to be free men."

"You already are, if you're English," said Peter.

"That," I said, "is what my pa says. He thinks of himself as an Englishman. I know he does."

"Was he born in England?"

"No, but my grandfather was."

"Where abouts?"

"Town of Suffolk," I said.

Peter shook his head. "I know it not. But to get back to what was early said, about the war, I mean, I pray there is none. Yet there will be. I feel it, too."

"How do you know?" asked Interest.

"A month ago, or less, we hanged a man here at Fort Ti. He was no older than I. Yet we saw him hang in our very court-yard. A Verdmont lad. I heard the officers quibble, divided as they were on his punishment. A smart flogging would have been enough, seeing as he was only pulling a prank."

"Like what?"

"Three boys tried to steal one of our cannon. No powder or ball, just the brass, but some of the officers called it an act of war. Sedition, they said. Had to teach the lad a lesson. A hanging is a sad thing to witness. They fell us out in ranks before the gallows and we all watched. Some of us wept. And if I think upon it much, I will weep again. Englishmen must not slay Englishmen."

"We are Americans now," I said. Interest nodded.

"And what you both tell me is that you would hang me, even though I am your friend. You would hang Private Geer?"

"Not I. Nor would Interest."

"But," said Interest, "there are those in our company who would. Like the man who near to poked your cheek with his musket, to prove his own bravery."

"Or lack of it," said our friend.

"These are times, I heard my father say, of sly passions. Our neighbor, family name of Haskin, is a Tory family. A week ago some fool burned their barn." I shook my head looking out over Lake Champlain. "We are not all neighbors as we used to be."

"Are the two of you going north with your leader? I overheard talk of Crown Point. It's twenty miles."

"You think I'd walk twenty more *steps* through that swamp? I druther go home," said Interest, "and farm it."

"Wouldn't mind," said Geer, "doing a little farming myself."

"Papa says there ain't no such thing as a little farming," I said. We all laughed.

"I wonder where he'll take us?" Peter let out a long breath.

"Who?"

"Your commandant, Colonel Allen. He can't leave us prisoners here at Ticonderoga no more than haul us north to Crown Point."

"You ever see Verdmont?" I asked him.

"Yes, of course." He pointed to the east, across Lake Champlain generally toward Interest Wheelock's homestead and to ours. "But only from here on the York side. More than once I'd yearn to set foot over there"

"Chapter, you thinking what I am?" said Interest.

"Yup, only not back through that swamp and all its bugs. Mister Geer, it don't do proper for a British soldier like yourself to pay call to America and not set down to a Verdmont breakfast."

"Or do a Verdmont day's work," said Interest.

"Can you swim, Peter?"

"Aye, like a sturgeon."

"Good," I said, "on account that it's only May, the waters of that lake are a mite cold and dark."

"So's a Yankee dungeon," Peter smiled. "Let's go."

We went. And run like three rabbits. Once in the water, we near to froze, and I never did warm up until two years later, which was the only day I ever could bear a short grudge against Peter Geer. And doggone, if Interest didn't darn near say the like. Both of us took a dram too much of rum that morning.

It was the day Peter wed Molly Painter.

ROBERT NEWTON PECK comes from a long row of Vermont farmers. His first novel was *A Day No Pigs Would Die*, followed by a nature book, *Path of Hunters*. His third book begins in Cornwall, Vermont, (1898) and is titled *Millie's Boy*. Then came *Soup* and more Vermont stories. His first historical novel was written about Fort Ticonderoga in the French and Indian War in 1758 entitled *Fawn*. Then came *Wild Cat*, more Soup stories called *Soup and Me*, a picture book for tots entitled *Hamilton*, and finally a book of poetry, *Bee Tree and Other Stuff*. His major novel on Ethan Allen will appear in early 1976, called *Hang For Treason*.

LAURA LYDECKER's first work appeared in *The New York Times* while she was still in school. She has done many book jackets, as well as illustrated books, *The Snow Rabbit* by Nancy Willard, plus Robert Newton Peck's *Hamilton* and *Bee Tree and Other Stuff*.

Peck and Lydecker both live in Darien, Connecticut.